Columbia University Lectures

James S. Carpentier Foundation

THE HISTORIANS OF ANGLO-AMERICAN LAW

BY

W. S. HOLDSWORTH

1927

THE HISTORIANS OF ANGLO-AMERICAN LAW

BY

W. S. HOLDSWORTH, K.C., D.C.L., Hon. LL.D.

VINERIAN PROFESSOR OF ENGLISH LAW
IN THE UNIVERSITY OF OXFORD

New York
COLUMBIA UNIVERSITY PRESS
1928

Set up and electrotyped. Published January 1928

PRINTED IN THE UNITED STATES OF AMERICA

CONTENTS

THE HISTORIANS OF ANGLO-AMERICAN LAW

I

THE PROFESSIONAL TRADITION

In the year 1888 the subject of Maitland's Inaugural Lecture, as Downing Professor of the Laws of England, was, "Why the History of English Law is not Written."[1] He answered the question somewhat as follows: the system of legal education evolved by the Inns of Court in the Middle Ages was a very good system as far as it went. It made "tough law," and "carried us safely from mediaeval to modern times." But "it could not produce its own historian"; and for this reason:

> "History involves comparison and the English lawyer who knew nothing and cared nothing for any system but his own hardly came in sight of the idea of legal history. And when the old scholastic plan of education broke down no other plan took its place. It is hardly too much to say that nobody taught law or attempted to teach it, and that no one studied law save with the most purely practical intentions. Whatever may be the advantages of such a mode of study it will never issue in a written history of English law."

At first sight, therefore, it would seem that there is little to say about the historians of Anglo-American law. But for three reasons I do not think that this conclusion follows from Maitland's lecture. In the first place, Maitland points out that, though no general history of English Law had then

[1] *Collected Papers*, i, 480.

been written, much historical work had been done on particular branches of the law — on constitutional law, on criminal law, and on the law of real property. In the second place, the continuity of English law has made it necessary that all lawyers should have some knowledge of the history of some branches of our law. At Maitland says,[2]

> "In his first text-book the student is solemnly warned that he must know the law as it stood in Edward I's day, and unfortunately it is quite impossible to write the simplest book about our land-law without speaking of the *De Donis* and the *Quia Emptores*. Well, a stranger might exclaim, what a race of medievalists you English lawyers ought to be! But on enquiry we shall find that the practical necessity for a little knowledge is a positive obstacle to the attainment of more knowledge, and also that what is really required of the practising lawyer is not, save in the rarest cases, a knowledge of medieval law as it was in the middle ages, but rather a knowledge of medieval law as interpreted by modern courts to suit modern facts."

That is not, it is true, the real historian's history; for it tends to pervert history by making it subservient to the necessity of proving the correctness of a modern legal principle. But, for all that, it keeps alive the necessity for learning law with an eye on history, and so preserves the historical point of view. In the third place, since 1888, the work of Maitland and of many other writers has done much to remove from Anglo-American law the reproach that its history has not been written. If Maitland could come to life to-day, I think that he would be the first to acknowledge joyfully that he would be obliged to re-write his lecture.

[2] *Collected Papers*, i, 490.

But, even in 1888, I think that much of the preliminary work, which is needed before a complete history of English law can be written, had been done — more perhaps than Maitland admitted. From the seventeenth century onwards, we have historical surveys of particular fields of English law; historians such as Spelman and Madox and Stubbs, who were not professional lawyers, had illuminated portions of our legal history; and many collections of legal documents, containing the raw materials for legal history, had been published — Rymer's Foedera, the Rolls of Parliament, the publications of the Record Commission, the publications in the Rolls Series, and the work of many societies, such as the Camden and the Surtees Societies. Moreover, in 1888, both in England and America, and in many continental countries, there had arisen a strong historical school of jurists, who were making a critical study, both of the work of the older lawyers, and of the new printed materials which were coming to be available. I think, therefore, that a survey of the work of some of the English and American lawyers, in the field of Anglo-American legal history, will help us both to understand the position which that study holds to-day, and to realize its importance to lawyers, to historians, and to statesmen.

We are told that we must look to the controversies of the Reformation period for the beginnings of true history. The search for authentic material which would support the theses of the contending parties, and the criticism which each party applied to the other's conclusions and to the materials on which they were based, begin the process which has given to history and to historical processes the scientific form which they have assumed to-day. In England we can see the beginnings of first-class historical research in the sixteenth and early seventeenth centuries. Lambard and Somner did good pioneer work upon the Anglo-Saxon laws; and, in the early seventeenth century, we can see in the members of the Antiquarian Society the men who, to use Maitland's phrase, made that period "the heroic age of English legal scholarship." [3] Among them were Sir Robert Cotton the great collector of records, and two of the earliest historians of our law — Selden and Hale. During the seventeenth and eighteenth centuries work continued to be done on the history of our law. At the end of the eighteenth and in the early nineteenth centuries the utilitarian school of law reformers, and their fellows, the upholders of the analytic school of jurisprudence, tended to turn men's thoughts from legal history. But the continuity of English institutions and law made it necessary for all English lawyers to know much legal history. The professional tradition, which the historical continuity of English law had necessarily imposed upon English lawyers, had been formed; and, like much else in English law, it had been given its classic and literate form by Blackstone. From the second half of the nineteenth century onwards a new school of historical lawyers took up the work of the historians of the seventeenth and eighteenth centuries, and began to develop the history of our law on broader lines. They were able to develop it on broader lines, first, because, under the influence of Maine and of continental writers, they had begun

[3] *Collected Papers*, iii, 453.

to realize that legal history, as Maitland put it, " involves comparison ";[4] and, secondly, because American historians had begun to show what great results can be obtained from a critical and scientific study of the early sources of our law. Much of the work of this new school of legal historians was summed up in Pollock and Maitland's classic history of English law which was first published in 1895. That history was largely the work of Maitland, who, more than any other single man in the whole course of our history, has restored the history of Anglo-American law to its rightful place, in relation both to English history and to English law. He was both a consummate lawyer and a consummate historian. Because he was a consummate lawyer he was initiated into that professional tradition, an acquaintance with which is a condition precedent to the writing of effective legal history; for, as he said,[5] " a thorough training in modern law is almost indispensable for any one who wishes to do good work on legal history. In whatever form the historian of law may give his results to the world . . . he will often have to work from the modern to the ancient, from the clear to the vague, from the known to the unknown." Because he was a consummate historian he knew how to distinguish between the historic truth taught by the authorities in an early period of the history of our law, and the legally correct doctrines which later ages had evolved from them.

This brief summary will indicate the scheme of these lectures. In this lecture I shall deal with the Professional Tradition of the historical development of English law,

[4] *Collected Papers*, i, 488.

[5] *Collected Papers*, i, 493.

which in many ways has influenced, and must continue to influence, the historians of Anglo-American law. In my second lecture I shall deal with the historians of the seventeenth and eighteenth centuries. In my third lecture I shall deal with the work of four Oxford professors of the nineteenth and twentieth centuries. In my fourth lecture I shall deal with the American and foreign contributions to our legal history. In my last lecture I shall say something of Maitland's life and work, and summarize the conclusions which can be drawn from the achievement of this long succession of historically minded men.

What I have called the Professional Tradition of the historical development of English law, could not develop till the law itself had come to depend on a series of authentic sources of some antiquity, and till the lawyers had come to use this series of sources to deduce historically the correct principles applicable to concrete cases. I do not think that this tradition was established much before the late sixteenth and early seventeenth centuries. In law, as in religion, the controversies of the period of the Reformation and Renaissance led to the attempt, by those who took different views on legal and political questions, to prove their theses by the authority of old precedents. I shall therefore begin by speaking briefly of what I shall call the prehistoric age. In the second place, I shall go on to speak of the establishment of the historical tradition in the late sixteenth and early seventeenth centuries. In the third place, I shall speak of its later history. Lastly, I shall say a few words of its effects on the study of legal history.

The Prehistoric Age

During this period, which covers the Middle Ages and some part of the sixteenth century, there are hardly any indications of the conscious use of legal history by practitioners, to define and establish the legal principles, which they lay down in text books, arguments, or decisions. What history there was takes, for the most part, the form of traditional legends; and those legends are generally used, rather to prove some political thesis, or merely to embellish an argument, than to establish the correctness of a legal proposition. Let us look at one or two illustrations:

Fortescue was a believer in the tale, invented by Geoffrey of Monmouth, that Brutus, the great grandson of Æneas, was the first king of the Britons;[6] and he seems to regard this legend as a proof of the antiquity of English law, which, he affirms, remained the same in spite of the conquests of the Romans, the Saxons, the Danes, and the Normans.[7] The author of that enigmatic composition, the Mirror of Justices, freely invented a series of tales as to the doings of King Alfred, in order to point his exposure of what he considered to be the abuses in the law of his own day.[8] In the fourteenth century some lawyers apparently believed the tale, told by counsel in 1307,[9] that there was a time when the king could be sued like an ordinary person;[10] and J.

[6] For this legend see Plummer's edition of *Fortescue's Governance of England,* 185–186.

[7] De Landibus, caps. 13 and 17.

[8] See Maitland's *Introduction to the Selden Society's Edition; cf.* Holdsworth, *H.E.L.* (3rd. Ed.), ii, 331.

[9] *Y.B.* 33–35 Ed., I (R.S.), 470.

[10] *Y.BB.* 22 Ed., III, pl. 25; 43 Ed., III, Mich., pl. 12.

Wilby even went so far as to say that he had seen a writ beginning *Praecipe Henrico Regi Angliae*[11] — if he had really seen such a writ it must have been, as Maitland says,[12] "some joke, some forgery, or possibly some relic of the Baron's War." Bacon rightly characterized these tales as "old fables."[13] In the latter part of the sixteenth century Plowden, in the Preface to his reports, recalled, or more probably invented, the tale that the Year Books were the work of official reporters paid by the King — a legend implicitly believed till the editors of the modern editions of the Year Books in the late nineteenth and twentieth centuries proved its baselessness.[14] But this, as we shall see, is a late instance and comes just before the establishment of the genuine historical tradition.

There are hardly any indications of the use of legal history to establish propositions of law. Fortescue states categorically propositions as to the powers of Parliament which, in the seventeenth century, gave rise to much historical argumentation. Littleton states his propositions of law equally categorically, and rarely lets us see any part of the historical scaffolding, by the help of which they were built up. Even in the few cases in which he notices differences of opinion, he gives us no historical argument in favour of one side or the other.[15] St. Germain, in his Doctor and Student, explains to us the reasons for the prevalence of uses; but, instead of giving us an historical explanation,

[11] *Y.B.* 24 Ed., III. Trin., pl. 40.
[12] P. and M. (1st Ed.) i. 500–501.
[13] *Case de Rege Inconsulto*, Works, vii, 694.
[14] Holdsworth, *H.E.L.* (3rd Ed.), ii, 532–536.
[15] See *e.g.*, § 10.

he gives us the results of his historical reading in a dogmatic form.[16] But, in spite of all these facts, I think that it is possible to maintain that the seeds of the professional tradition of the historical development of the law were sown in this prehistoric age. That they were then sown is, I think, due to the gradual evolution of the system of case law. The Year Books show us that the reports of cases were becoming the main source of the unenacted law. It is true that the conditions of the publication of these reports before the invention of printing, and the peculiarities of mediaeval procedure, cause the reports in the Year Books to differ from the modern reports; and the authority of the Year Book cases to differ from the authority of the cases in the modern reports. But it is clear that, from the beginning of the fourteenth century, respect was paid to the decisions of the courts; and it is clear from the later Year Books, and from the arguments in Plowden's Reports, that that respect was on the increase. Obviously, as that respect increases, both the bar and the bench will tend more and more to trace back the history of a principle through the cases, in order to establish its correctness. We shall now see that it was the growth of this practice, which was the chief cause for the establishment of the professional tradition of the historical development of English law at the end of the sixteenth and the beginning of the seventeenth centuries.

The Establishment of an Historical Tradition

In the latter part of the sixteenth and at the end of the seventeenth centuries, there were three main reasons for the

[16] *Doctor and Student,* Bk. II, c. 22.

establishment of this professional tradition of the historical development of English law.

In the first place, in the new age of Reformation and Renaissance it was necessary in England, as in many European countries, to adapt mediaeval rules to modern needs. In most European countries this adaptation took the form of a Reception of Roman law of varying degrees of intensity. No such Reception took place in England. Instead, the rules of the mediaeval common law were adapted to the new situation; and, where they were inadequate, new courts and councils, administering special bodies of law, were either newly created, or assumed a new activity. Both these methods of bringing the law into line with the new conditions resulted in placing a new emphasis upon historical considerations. The adaptation of the rules of the mediaeval common law to modern conditions involved the application of a process of selection and rejection to the mass of scattered, and often inconsistent, dicta to be found in the printed Year Books and Abridgments. It is clear from the arguments, which Plowden elaborately reported, that this often took the form of an historical arrangement of the authorities upon which counsel relied. The activities of the new courts and councils, such as the Chancery, the court of Requests, the Admiralty, the Star Chamber, and the provincial councils of Wales and the North, were raising, at the end of the sixteenth century, questions as to the limits of the jurisdiction of these courts, and of their relation to the common law courts. These questions necessarily involved historical research into the origins of these courts. Famous illustrations are the controversies as to the legality of the jurisdiction of the Star Chamber, of the provincial councils of Wales and the North, and of the court of Requests. But this is closely allied to the second of the reasons for the establishment of this professional tradition.

In the second place, at the end of the sixteenth century, there are signs that these controversies as to jurisdiction will merge in more fundamental political and constitutional questions. There are signs that the days of the balanced Tudor polity, which left large and undefined powers to King, Council, Parliament and the law, were numbered; and that some more definite settlement between powers, which were becoming rivals, was needed. The accession of the house of Stuart, and the clear cut theories of James I as to the extent of his prerogative, precipitated all these questions of public law. Two different theories of the state — the Parliamentary and the Royalist — emerged; and both Parliament and the Crown appealed to historical arguments. As Maitland has said, "Great questions were opening, and on all sides an appeal was being made to ancient law and ancient history." [17]

In the third place, the study of history for its own sake, and on something like scientific lines, was beginning. I have already mentioned Lambard and Somner's work on the Anglo-Saxon laws; and Lambard's work on the Justices of the Peace, and on the central courts, is marked both by historical research, and by the careful and accurate use which he made of the work of his predecessors. Bacon,

[17] *Collected Papers*, iii, 453.

whose history of Henry VII gives him some claims to be called the first of our modern historians,[18] included in his scheme for digesting the laws of England a book *De antiquitatibus juris.*[19]

For all these reasons arguments based upon history played a large part in the complicated process of making the mediaeval common law fit to guide the life of the modern English state. It was inevitable, therefore, that a professional tradition of the historical development of the law should grow up. The form which that professional tradition would take depended on the issue of those great questions of public law which divided the state in the seventeenth century. If the Stuart kings and the prerogative lawyers had prevailed, it would have been a tradition very different from that which we know to-day. Because Parliament, in alliance with the common lawyers, gained the victory, it was shaped by the man who embodied the ideals of both — Edward Coke. He did more than any other single man to shape the professional tradition of the common law, partly because he was the most profound common lawyer of his day, partly because he became in his later years a leader of the Parliamentary party, and partly because he had provided in his Reports and Institutes a complete and up to date survey of the principles and rules of English law. The

[18] Spedding, *Letters and Life*, vii, 302, says of this work, "Every history which has been written since has derived all its light from this, and followed its guidance in every question of importance; and the additional materials which come to light from time to time, and enable us to make many corrections in the history of the events, only serve to confirm and illustrate the truth of its interpretation of them."

[19] Spedding, *Letters and Life*, vi, 68.

result was that, when the Parliamentary party triumphed after 1641, lawyers and politicians alike accepted his statements as not only authoritative, but almost infallible.

Now Coke was not a true historian. He was always the lawyer, always the advocate, and, in his later years, a keen politician. These defects have done two very real disservices to the professional tradition of the historical development of English law. In the first place, this mental attitude made him uncritical in the use of his authorities. It led him to use any argument, strong or weak, which might affect the decision. For instance, he swallowed whole the statements made in the Mirror of Justices, and, by his credulity, gave it currency as a serious law book. He accepted all its statements because they confirmed his preconceived ideas as to the antiquity of the common law, and confirmed his theory that the common law owed little or nothing to William the Conqueror and his successors. Similarly, he accepted the old legends about Brutus, and seems to have convinced himself that the ancient Britons talked Greek.[20] Coke thus passed on into the professional tradition of the modern common law many of the legends current in the prehistoric era of our law. In the second place, in matters of public law he adopted the attitude of a politician; and in discussing the jurisdiction of rival courts he adopted the attitude of a fanatical common lawyer. He has, in these respects, perverted history by leading future historians to believe that the law on these matters was clear, and that the principles upon which the Parliamentary statesmen acted were always correct.

[20] 3 Co. Rep., Pref., viii–ix.

On the other hand, I cannot doubt that Coke's services in starting a sound professional tradition outweigh these defects. In matters unconnected with the political and professional controversies of the day, on some questions of public law and on many questions of purely private law, he does deduce modern law from the old authorities in a masterly fashion. "Out of the old fields must grow the new corn" was a motto which he several times repeats; and there is no doubt that, both in his Reports and in his Institutes, he did skilfully use the Year Books and other mediaeval authorities, and the modern cases, to construct a definite body of modernized rules. Let us recall the testimony of Bacon — his great professional rival and his political opponent. "Had it not been for Sir Edward Coke's reports the law of this time had almost been like a ship without ballast; for that the cases of modern experience are fled from those that are adjudged and ruled in former times."[21] Coke's writings, by preserving the essential continuity of the common law in this age of transition, established an historical tradition which was for the most part sound. No doubt his uncritical use of authority, and his political bias, did grave injury to some parts of that tradition — it perpetuated legends, and it perpetuated a biassed view of constitutional law. But in most departments of the law it gave the profession a sound tradition. Let us recall the opinion of Charles Butler — the great conveyancer and real property lawyer of the eighteenth and early nineteenth centuries. He said that he had "never met with a person thoroughly conversant in the law of real property who did not think

[21] Spedding, *Letters and Life*, vi, 65.

with him — that *he* is the best lawyer, and will succeed best in his profession, who best understands Coke upon Littleton." [22] We shall now see that the fact that this historical tradition of the common law, which Coke founded, was in the main sound, is best proved by its later history.

The Later History

During the latter part of the seventeenth, during the eighteenth, and during the nineteenth centuries, the historical tradition grew in strength and in purity. During all these centuries it has given every sound lawyer some tincture of legal history, and it has made some of our more learned lawyers no mean historians. Let us glance briefly at the evidence for these statements.

The middle and latter part of the seventeenth century can claim Sir Mathew Hale — the greatest of our legal historians before Maitland. I shall deal fully with his work in my next lecture. Here it will be sufficient to say that his great work on the Pleas of the Crown, did much for the professional tradition of the historical development of the criminal law; and that some of his other works, notably his book on the Jurisdiction of the House of Lords, did a similar service for parts of our constitutional law. In fact, the result of the great constitutional controversies of the early part of the century was both to elucidate many points of constitutional law, and to impress upon lawyers the need to study this and other branches of the law historically. Roger North tells us that his brother Francis, who became Lord Keeper Guildford, had discovered, in the course of his

[22] *Reminiscences*, i, 65.

historical researches, the truth, which is now universally admitted, that mediaeval precedents were by no means conclusively in favour of all the claims made by Parliament. He studied the records; and had transcripts made for him with a view to the composition of a history of Parliaments.[23] He was by no means a solitary student; and this more intensive study of legal history had important constitutional results. It made it difficult for James II to get twelve judges, and impossible for him to get twelve lawyers, who would see eye to eye with him on political questions.

The improvement in the character of the bench, which followed on the Revolution, considerably strengthened the professional tradition of the historical development of the law. This fact can be illustrated, first, from cases in which the judges used their historical learning to resist innovations upon settled doctrines of the common law; and, secondly, from cases in which they developed, from old rules and old ideas, the new rules which changed conditions demanded, without any essential breach in the historical continuity of legal doctrine.

The best illustration of the first point — the manner in which the judges used their historical learning to resist innovations upon settled doctrines of the common law — is to be found in the way in which they dealt with the legal heresies of Lord Mansfield. Lord Mansfield was perhaps the greatest legal genius of the eighteenth century; and his achievements in many branches of the common law — notably in the sphere of mercantile law — have played no small part in the work of adapting the common law to mod-

[23] *Lives of the Norths*, i, 353–355.

ern conditions. He had a prophetic eye for the manner in which the law ought to be modified to meet those conditions; and, being learned in other systems of law besides the common law, he was not oppressed by an undue reverence for all its technical rules. These qualities led him to attempt to pervert the historical tradition of the common law in order to secure results which seemed to him to be desirable. Like many other eighteenth century lawyers and thinkers, he was firmly impressed with the idea that the age in which he lived was the most enlightened age in the history of England; and that, since a great many of the binding precedents of the common law came from a barbarous, or, as the phrase then was, a " Gothic " age, they ought, if possible, to be moulded to meet the ideas of this age of enlightenment. This led him to attempt to reduce the rule in *Shelley's Case*[24] to the level of a mere rule of construction;[25] to attempt to reform the law as to seisin and disseisin by a theory as to the meaning of those terms for which there was no English authority;[26] to attempt to reform the law of contract by reducing the doctrine of consideration to a position of very minor importance;[27] and to attempt to get rid of the inconvenience of the separation between law and equity by giving recognition to equitable rights in a court of law.[28]

[24] " Things were not going well with the rule. Its feudal origin was a disgrace. Its antiquity was a reproach. Some judges thought that on those grounds it ought to be discountenanced," *per* Lord Macnaghten, Foxwell v. Van Grutten [1897]. *A.C.* at p. 669.

[25] Perrin v. Blake (1770), 4 Burr. 2579, and *Collect. Jurid.*, 283; S.C. on appeal (1772), 1 W., *Blackstone,* 673 *n.; cp.* Holdsworth, *H.E.L.* (3rd Ed.), iii, 109–110.

[26] See Holdsworth, *H.E.L.*, vii, 43–44.

[27] *Ibid.*, viii, 29–30. [28] *Ibid.*, vii, 19–20.

The Legislature in the nineteenth century has indorsed the wisdom of Lord Mansfield's endeavours to reform the law by enacting statutes which embody the substance of most of his ideas. The new Property Acts have abolished the rule in *Shelley's Case*. Nineteenth century legislation has reformed the law as to seisin and disseisin on lines which Lord Mansfield would have approved. The Judicature Acts fused the courts of law and equity. Perhaps some day the doctrine of consideration will be reformed on the lines which Lord Mansfield would have approved. But all these reforms were reforms of a character which could only be made by the Legislature. It is possible for a great judge, as Lord Mansfield's work in the sphere of mercantile law proved, to make new law when the existing principles are nebulous and the rules scanty. It is not possible for the greatest of judges to innovate in those departments of law in which the principles are ascertained and the rules precise. And so, in all these cases, the professional tradition was successful in resisting Lord Mansfield's innovations, because it had absorbed sufficient history to prove conclusively that his decisions were not law.

But, in the second place, though this tradition resisted innovations, which could be proved historically not to be law, it was by no means a blindly conservative tradition. In the eighteenth century, as in preceding centuries, it combined a sense of historical continuity with a recognition of the need to keep the law abreast of the needs of the age. The system of case law, by means of which it worked, insured this combination of qualities; for the facts of the cases which came before the courts kept the lawyers in touch with the needs of the age, and the need to deduce the rule from the decisions in previous cases preserved an historical continuity. There are many illustrations of the way in which the judges thus expanded the law on truly historical lines. One of the best is the judgment of C. J. Parker in 1711 in the case of *Mitchel v. Reynolds* [29] — the case which is the starting point of the development of the modern law as to contracts in restraint of trade. In his judgment C. J. Parker reviewed the whole subject of restraints on trade. These restraints, he pointed out, might be either involuntary or voluntary. The mediaeval restraints were involuntary — they were imposed by charters, customs, or bylaws. The new restraints were voluntary — they were imposed by the agreement of the parties. Just as the mediaeval law had recognised that some of these involuntary restraints were good, provided that they were reasonable, so modern law should recognise that a reasonable voluntary restraint was good. Out of the old fields, as Coke had put it, the new corn was made to grow. In the use which C. J. Parker made of the analogy of the mediaeval involuntary restraints, depending on charters, customs and bylaws, we see a skilful adaptation of some of the principles underlying semi-obsolete modes of controlling trade, to the needs of a new age, in which it was desirable to allow a greater freedom to trade. The principle that all restraints on trade must be justified by reasonableness was taken over from the mediaeval law, and new tests of reasonableness suited to the new age were evolved.

Thus, throughout the eighteenth century, the profes-

[29] 1 P. Wms, 181; *cp.* Holdsworth, *H.E.L.*, viii, 60–62.

sional tradition of historic continuity was preserved and strengthened. In the third quarter of that century it was broadened and enlightened by the publication of Blackstone's Commentaries. Of Blackstone as a legal historian I shall speak more at length in my next lecture, when I am dealing with the legal historians of the seventeenth and eighteenth centuries; for his Commentaries are not only a statement of the law of Blackstone's day, but the best history of English law as a whole which had yet appeared. At this point, I only mention the Commentaries to point out that the skilful manner in which Blackstone uses his authorities new and old, and the analogy of other systems of law, to illustrate the evolution of the law of his day, had a vast influence, both in England and America, in implanting in the profession a sound tradition of the historical development of the law. The Commentaries began the process of eliminating many of those crude legends of the prehistoric age, to which Coke's credulity had given currency, and of substituting for them a reasoned and a rational history. The fact that they had this result was of the utmost service to English law in the new age of reform which opened shortly after Blackstone's death.

The complacent satisfaction with things established, and the tendency to regard other ages as uncivilized and "Gothic" by comparison, which characterized so much of the thought of the eighteenth century, tended to make men undervalue the teachings of history. We have seen that this fact is illustrated by some of Lord Mansfield's heresies. But, in Lord Mansfield's day, it was on all hands admitted that historical learning was necessary to understand the true meaning of the excellent law and institutions of England. It is clear, however, that if this belief in the excellence of that law and those institutions was shaken, and if at the same time the tendency to regard the ideas of the present age as the most enlightened that the world had yet seen continued to exist, the way would be prepared for a philosophy of law which had little use for history, legal or otherwise. That is what happened at the end of the eighteenth century. The industrial revolution, the influence of the ideas propagated by the French revolution, and the influence of the ideas propagated by Bentham and his rationalistic followers, shattered the eighteenth century belief in the excellence of the laws and institutions of England; and reformers of various kinds were not prepared to admit that they needed any help from the comparatively barbarous ages of the past to invent the reforms which were needed.

Bentham and his followers shaped the course of law reform in England. Their programme, and the postulate on which it was based, can be stated in a sentence. They proposed to submit all institutions and all laws to the test of utility — the greatest happiness of the greatest number; and they assumed that men's actions and instincts at all times and in all places were fundamentally the same. Utility, as Sir Leslie Stephen said, was to them " a kind of permanent and ultimate entity which is the same at all periods." [30] And so Bentham was prepared to " legislate for Hindoostan as well as for his own parish; and to make codes not only for England, Spain, and Russia, but for Morocco." [31] It is true that he admitted that we must allow

[30] *The English Utilitarians,* i, 302. [31] *Ibid.*, 300.

for circumstances such as climate, beliefs, or customs; but "the real assumption is that all such circumstances are superficial, and can be controlled and altered indefinitely by the Legislature." [32] Bentham and his school were assisted in coming to these conclusions by the fact that they fixed their attention only on the world as they then saw it, and only on the individual persons in that world. They neglected all the complex social evolution which had gone to the making of that world and to the individuals in it. It is for this reason that they considered that the study of history was a matter of minor importance.[33] The only uses they assigned to it were, first, its use in giving a series of illustrations of the errors of less enlightened ages; and, secondly, its use in providing evidence for the universal laws for the guidance of human activities, which they thought that they had discovered. Of this second use, which they assigned to history, I must give a few words of explanation.

The great advances in the discovery of universal laws governing inanimate nature, which were being made at the end of the eighteenth and the beginning of the nineteenth centuries, induced this rationalistic school to think that laws regulating all human activities could be discovered and stated, which were as universally true as the laws regulating inanimate nature. Law, economics, and history were all to

[32] *Ibid.*

[33] "The fatal tendency of rationalistic thought towards the simplification of experience by the isolation of the single individual, explains the indifference and even hostility towards the principal source of social experience, namely, history. The latter is not only ignored, but treated with hatred and contempt, as a source of superstition and mischievous authority," Vinogradoff, *Historical Jurisprudence,* i, 108.

become exact sciences. In the sphere of law this led to the analytical school of jurisprudence founded by Austin — there was to be a formal science of positive law based upon the principles and rules of mature legal systems. In the sphere of economics this led to the growth of the classical political economy. In the sphere of history it led to Buckle's ambitious attempt to write a history of civilization which was to prove the existence and working of these scientific laws.

We shall see in a subsequent lecture that, in the middle of the nineteenth century, a new school of historical lawyers arose. But, till they arose, these *a priori* ideas held the field, and, though they did not prevent, they tended to discourage any great work on legal history. It was in these adverse conditions that the professional tradition of the historical development of the law, as broadened and enlightened by Blackstone, was of the utmost service to the cause of historical continuity. Large parts of English law were reformed by men who had learned in Bentham's school. But the reformers were lawyers bred up in the professional tradition; and the reforms were generally preceded by reports which contained careful historical statements of the law, reasons why reforms were needed, and skilful suggestions as to how the new rules could, with least disturbance, be substituted for the old. The Fines and Recoveries Act is a striking illustration of the manner in which a mass of complicated procedural rules were swept away with the minimum of change in the substantive principles of the law. I have elsewhere shown that some of the reforms in the law of pleading actually tended to recall older rules of law, which the rationalism of the eighteenth century had slurred over or ignored; and that, in consequence, those older rules played some part in the settlement of the modern form of the doctrine of consideration, and in some other modern rules of law.[34] All through the century, and down to the present day, the maintenance of this historical tradition can be seen in the judgments of great lawyers such as Willes, Blackburn, Cockburn, Bowen, and Macnaghten.

I must now consider the effects of this professional tradition on the study of our legal history.

The Effects of the Professional Tradition

Maitland, as we have seen,[35] has emphasized one of the bad effects of this tradition. The lawyer looks at law from the point of view of its bearing on the case before him. He reads his mediaeval authorities with the object, not of finding out what they meant for the lawyer of the Middle Ages, but of finding out what they have come to mean in the light of more modern decisions. "It is possible," as Maitland says,[36] "to find in modern books comparisons between what Bracton says and what Coke says about the law as it stood before the statutes of Edward I, and the writer of course tells us that Coke's is 'the better opinion.' Now if we want to know the common law of our own day Coke's authority is higher than Bracton's, and Coke's own doctrines yield easily to modern decisions. But if we are really looking for the law of Henry III's reign, Bracton's lightest word is infinitely more valuable than all the tomes of Coke. A

[34] *Cambridge Law Journal*, i, 273–277.
[35] Above, 4. [36] *Collected Papers*, i, 491.

mixture of legal dogma and legal history is in general an unsatisfactory compound."

Another of its bad effects is to obscure the need for a comparison of our law with the law of other countries. The law of mediaeval France, for instance, can be made to shed much light upon the law of mediaeval England by reason both of its similarities and its contrasts. Take the history of the jury. Why did it fade out in France and develop in England? The answer to that question gives us valuable lights upon many aspects of the history of the English system of procedure civil and criminal. But the professional tradition is apt, unless it is recalled to better ways by such a book as Blackstone's Commentaries, to attend only to its own insular development as portrayed in its insular statutes and decisions.

In spite, however, of these drawbacks I should contend that the maintenance of this professional tradition has had, on the whole, beneficial effects on the study of legal history.

In the first place, it has driven into the minds of all practising lawyers, who wish to be something more than mere practitioners, the essential fact that they must study some legal history if they are to attain that mastery of the law which comes of understanding. Roger North put this very well in the sentence which I have placed on the title page of my History of English Law — " To say truth, although it is not necessary for counsel to know what the history of a point is, but to know how it now stands resolved, yet it is a wonderful accomplishment, and, without it, a lawyer can not be accounted learned in the law." [37]

[37] *A Discourse on the Study of the Laws*, 40.

In the second place, we have seen that Maitland emphasized the fact that the historian of law must know modern law — he must know the end of the story.[38] An editor of Year Books, for instance, must know enough of the law of the sixteenth and of later centuries to be able to see in the dicta of the bench and bar the beginnings of new and fruitful ideas. Dicta of this kind have far more historical importance than the many pages in the Year Books devoted to those wrangles about minute points in the procedure in the real actions. I think that a lawyer who has the professional tradition is, for that reason, better fitted to be an editor of Year Books than a historian or a lawyer whose legal learning is entirely mediaeval. In other words, the professional tradition has gone a long way to fitting him to be a legal historian.

In the third place, the fact that our system of case law has compelled lawyers to go from precedent to precedent, means that they are often obliged to discuss and distinguish cases from all periods in our legal history. The result is that the reports not only contain summaries of the history of a point at different periods, but also the authorities on which those summaries are based. These summaries, as I can testify from my own experience, are of the utmost value to the legal historian. It is true that they are made for a purpose — for the purpose of deciding the issues raised by the pleadings. It is true that they are sometimes based on false historical traditions. But it is equally true that they always give the historian a starting point, which easily leads him to other authorities, and eventually to a

[38] Above, 7.

conclusion as to the course of the true historical development.

The professional tradition as to the historical development of English law is an element with which all its historians must reckon. We can easily guard ourselves from being misled by the two drawbacks to which it is subject; and, for the three reasons which I have just given, I think that it has, on the whole, smoothed the path of the legal historian.

In this lecture I have been dealing with the almost unconscious contribution made to the study of our legal history by men whose main object was to master modern law. In my next two lectures I shall deal with the conscious contribution made to the study of our legal history by certain English historians and lawyers, whose main object was to elucidate the historical development of the law.

II

THE HISTORIANS OF THE SEVENTEENTH AND EIGHTEENTH CENTURIES

THE latter part of the sixteenth and the beginning of the seventeenth centuries is the greatest of all periods in the history of English literature. The literary activity of that period affected many branches of learning, and not the least historical learning. The age of Shakespeare and Bacon was also, in Maitland's opinion, the heroic age of English legal and historical scholarship.[1] In the work of men like Lambard, in the work of the band of scholars who formed the Antiquarian Society,[2] we see the beginnings of the study of the history of many sides of English life — legal and otherwise — on scientific lines. These men founded a lasting tradition of historical scholarship, which has had an enduring influence on the future studies of many varieties of historians from that day to this.

We are here concerned with the history of our law. But law touches life on many sides, so that it is sometimes diffi-

[1] *Collected Papers*, iii, 453.

[2] This Society was founded in 1572 largely by the encouragement of Archbishop Parker. Cotton was elected in 1590, and it met for many years at his house. It ceased to meet regularly after 1604. In 1717 a new Society was founded by men of historical learning who had met informally since 1707. In 1770 the Society began to print some of its papers under the title of Archaeologia. *Cambridge History of Literature*, ix, 357–358; Nichols, *Literary Anecdotes*, vi, 140–160.

cult to put into mutually exclusive classes legal and non-legal historians. Many historians, who cannot be classed as strictly legal historians, have dealt largely with legal history, and have laid the foundations for the historical study of many of its aspects. We must not neglect these writers to whom the historians of Anglo-American law have owed and still owe so great a debt. I shall therefore deal first with some of these writers, whom I shall call the border-line legal historians; and then I shall deal more at length with the men whose work places them definitely in the category of legal historians.

The Border-line Historians

During the latter part of the sixteenth century, during the whole of the seventeenth century, and during the earlier part of the eighteenth century, the work of some of these historians is very important. It comprises many matters cognate to legal history; and the books which they wrote all were, some still are, the chief authorities upon these matters. We can trace their influence in four main directions. First, there is the group of writers who restored the study of the Anglo-Saxon language, literature, and laws. Secondly, there is the larger group of writers who deal with the history of legal institutions in many different ways, and from many different points of view. Thirdly, there is the smaller group of writers whose work touches upon the history of legal doctrine. Fourthly, there are the writers who have helped the legal historian by printing and publishing collections of original documents.

(1) The Anglo-Saxon group

The work of this group of scholars had both a positive and a negative significance. It had a positive significance because, by reviving the study of the Anglo-Saxon language and restoring the text of the Anglo-Saxon laws, it enabled scholars to reach some assured conclusions as to facts of Anglo-Saxon history and the contents of the Anglo-Saxon laws. It had a negative significance because it showed up the absurdity of the fables, such as those invented by the author of the *Mirror of Justices*, which, in the prehistoric age, had been substituted for authentic history. It is true that some of these fables had yet a long life before them. But it was the work of this group of men which supplied the materials for their exposure.

The most famous name in this group is William Lambard.[3] He was born in 1536. He was called to the bar by Lincoln's Inn in 1567, and became a bencher of that Society in 1579. In the same year he was made justice of the peace for Kent. In 1592 he became a master in Chancery, in 1597 keeper of the rolls at the house of the rolls in Chancery Lane, and in 1601 the keeper of the records in the Tower. He died in the same year. But he signalized his single year of office as keeper of the records in the Tower by cataloguing them. This catalogue he presented to Queen Elizabeth at a personal interview, at which she read the catalogue and had it explained to her by Lambard. After a curious conversation about Richard II, in which she made some veiled allusions to Essex's rebellion, she expressed her great satisfaction at

[3] *D.N.B.*; Holdsworth, *H.E.L.*, iv, 117–118, v, 403; *cp.* Putnam, *Early Treatises upon the Justice of the Peace*, 215–221.

the work; and, says Lambard, " being called away to prayer, she put the book in her bosom, having forbidden me from first to last to fall upon my knee before her — concluding, 'Farewell, good and honest Lambard.' "[4]

This was a happy conclusion to a long life of historical toil and public service; for Lambard was an historian and an antiquary as well as a lawyer. It is his writings on legal history with which we are here concerned. These writings, which he called by anglicized Greek names, were the *Archaionomia* — the edition of the Anglo-Saxon laws; the *Archeion* — an historical commentary on the central courts of justice in England; and the *Eirenarcha* — a treatise on the justices of the peace, to which he added a small tract on constables and other humbler officials of the country. Of the two last named works I shall speak when I deal with the group of books on legal institutions. The *Archaionomia*, which was published in 1568, restored the Anglo-Saxon laws to the students of the common law; and, considering that he was " a pioneer in an unknown land "[5] his work was, in Liebermann's opinion, wonderfully good.

Another pioneer in this field was Somner (1598–1669)[6] — an ecclesiastical lawyer and the son of an ecclesiastical

[4] " He presented her Majestie with his Pandecta of all her rolls, bundells, membranes, and parcells, that be reposed in her Majesties Tower at London; whereof she had given to him the charge 21st Jan. last past. Her Majestie cheerfullie received the same into her hands, saying, 'You intended to present this book by the Countesse of Warwicke; but I will none of that: for if any subject of mine do me a service I will thankfully accept it at his hands,' " Nichols, *Bibliotheca Topographica*. i. App. VII. pp. 525–526.

[5] Maitland. *Collected Papers*. iii. 453.

[6] Holdsworth, *H.E.L.*, v, 403–404.

lawyer. He did valuable work in the allied departments of Anglo-Saxon language and literature, and the antiquities of legal history. Of his work in the second of these departments I shall speak later. In the first of these departments he wrote some observations on the Laws of Henry I, made a translation, which he did not publish, of Lambard's Latin text of the Anglo-Saxon laws, and translated Anglo-Saxon documents for Dugdale's Monasticon. His most important work was his Saxon-Latin-English Dictionary, to help in the publication of which John Spelman gave him the income of the Anglo-Saxon lectureship, which his father Henry Spelman had founded at Cambridge. Henry Spelman, of whose work I shall speak later, was also an Anglo-Saxon scholar, as his Glossary shows;[7] and, in the seventeenth and eighteenth centuries, the works of Wheelock (1644), Hicks the nonjuring bishop (1703–5), and Wilkins (1721) show that the study was still alive. But, in the latter part of the eighteenth century and in the earlier half of the nineteenth century, general interest in these laws waned; and there was no great revival of interest till the rise of the modern historical school in the nineteenth century, of which I shall speak in a later lecture.

At this point I must try to answer three questions: first, what was the cause of this interest in the history and laws of the Anglo-Saxons: secondly, what influence did the work of this group of men have upon the study of legal history: and, thirdly, why did this branch of study suffer a decline at the end of the eighteenth century.

First, the original cause of this interest in Anglo-Saxon

[7] Holdsworth, *H.E.L.*, v, 401–402, 404.

literature and law was largely, to use Maitland's phrase "a by-product of the Reformation."[8] The Anglican church, according to Henry VIII's theory, was the old Catholic church which had purified itself by getting rid of the "usurped" jurisdiction of the Pope, and of Roman abuses. A study of the Anglo-Saxon laws might help to prove the truth of this thesis. "It seemed possible that, expressed in an unknown tongue and a barely legible script, there lay title deeds of a national church, — title deeds which told not only of independence, but of purity."[9] Later on, when the constitutional controversies began to become acute, the Paliamentarians and common lawyers thought that in the Anglo-Saxon laws there could be found the title deeds of the constitution. Even Lambard seems to have thought that the Parliament could be traced back to Anglo-Saxon days.[10] Coke and the common lawyers considered that these Anglo-Saxon days were the golden age of freedom; that this golden age had declined when the Norman Conquest had brought in alien laws and an alien servitude; and that Parliament, an institution of that golden age, was attempting to get rid of the effects of the Norman Conquest, and to bring back again the old freedom. "To speak what we think," said Coke,[11] "we would derive from the Conqueror as little as we could." Even Hale thought it incumbent on him to spend time, in his short History of the Common Law, on the question in what sense, if at all, William I could be said to be a conqueror. He felt that he must maintain the unbroken pedigree of the English constitution and English

[8] *Collected Papers,* iii, 452.
[9] *Ibid.*
[10] *Archeion* (Ed. 1635), 242–259.
[11] *Third Instit.,* Preface.

law from the period before the Conquest.[12] And Blackstone gives countenance to the theory that, in the Saxon period, the English constitution and English law had attained a perfection, which had been spoilt by the tyrannous laws of the Norman kings, and was only gradually restored in succeeding ages.[13]

Secondly, what influence did the work of this group of men have on the study of legal history? I cannot but think that this use of the Anglo-Saxon law and history has, in many respects been of disservice to the cause of legal history. The question, to what extent the Anglo-Saxon laws and Anglo-Saxon institutions influenced the making of the common law and the English constitution, is in truth a complex historical problem which is even now not completely solved. To drag a problem of this kind into the arena of ecclesiastical and political controversy was just the way to retard the attainment of a conclusion; and, in fact, it is the cessation of this manner of conducting these controversies which, in our days, has at length caused scientific historians, who have attempted to solve the problems on the right lines, to be heard with increasing respect. On the other hand, though a controversial and therefore an unhistorical use was made of this Anglo-Saxon material, it did help genuine historical students to see a little way into the misty period before the Conquest. Selden, in his two tracts on Probate and Grants of Administration, and Somner in his treatise on gavelkind, made an intelligent use of Anglo-Saxon evidence. And the use of this evidence will tend to discountenance the old

[12] *History of the Common Law* (6th Ed.), 94-126.
[13] *Comm.*, iv, 420.

fables told in such books as the *Mirror of Justices.* It is true that Blackstone still professes a belief in the perfections of the English constitution in the Saxon period, and that he cites the *Mirror:* but he makes no extensive use of that work; and Reeves, who, as we shall see, wrote at the end of the eighteenth century, regarded the *Mirror* with suspicion.[14]

Thirdly, why did this branch of study suffer a decline at the end of the eighteenth century? It is largely because lawyers and historians were beginning to get a more accurate knowledge of the Anglo-Saxon period that the study of the Anglo-Saxon laws declined at the end of the eighteenth century. The ecclesiastical and constitutional controversies of the sixteenth and seventeenth centuries were settled; and men were beginning to see that many of the arguments based on Anglo-Saxon history were worthless. Lawyers found the Anglo-Saxon laws incomprehensible; and they could comfort themselves with the thought that, as they dated from before the time of legal memory, no great stress need be laid upon them. The records of the period after that time were easier to read and more profitable as precedents. As Maitland says,[15] these old laws " had disappointed reasonable expectations. . . . What is one to make of laws which leave it somewhat doubtful whether our Saxon forefathers were possessed of our glorious constitution, with trial by jury, and habeas corpus, and all other bulwarks, palladia, checks, balances, commodities, easements, and appurtenances? " And so it happened that it is not till the revival of historical

[14] *H.E.L.*, ii, 232-238 (Finlason's Ed.).
[15] *Collected Papers*, iii, 454-455.

studies, and the growth of a school of scientific legal historians in the nineteenth century, that these old laws were again studied, and studied in the right way — not in order to prove a case, but in order to discover their real meaning, and the exact extent of their influence upon the development of English law.

(*2*) *Writers on the history of legal institutions*

This is a very large group. In the sixteenth century there are Lambard's two works — the *Archeion* on central, and the *Einrenarcha* on local government. The *Archeion* was completed in 1596, but was not published till 1635. It is an able historical summary of the position of the courts of common law, and of those newer courts and councils which had been developing so rapidly in the sixteenth century. It shows how hazy the relations of all those courts new and old were to each other in the Tudor period; and, as we might expect from a Tudor lawyer, Lambard is inclined to give to the Council a large discretionary power. I think that its main historical interest is to be found in the fact that it gives us the view of a literary and historically minded man, who was writing in the period before the conflicts between these rival courts had become matters of acute political controversy. The *Einrenarcha* is perhaps Lambard's most learned legal work.[16] In it he both used and digested the large mass of literature on the justices of the peace. Moreover I think that we can say that, for the first and only time

[16] For an account of a MS. containing (*inter alia*) the earliest form of the MS. of the first two books of the 1581–2 edition of the *Einrenarcha*, and for an account of the relation of this edition to the later editions, see Miss Putnam's note in *E.H.R.*, xli, 260–273.

in the history of this literature, he gave it a literary form. His book was a vast improvement on all the books which had preceded it; and, shortly after, writers on this subject abandoned all attempt to give it a literary form, and had recourse to an alphabetical arrangement.

In the earlier part of the seventeenth century the political controversies produced a large literature. One of the leading figures was Prynne (1600–1669). His career is astonishing. He was mutilated and imprisoned by the Star Chamber for his attacks on the king, queen, and bishops. He was a distinguished member of the Long Parliament. He was an opponent of the army, and was imprisoned for three years without trial under the Commonwealth. He supported the Restoration, and became a recognised authority upon constitutional law and Parliamentary procedure. He ended his life as keeper of the records in the Tower; and he lived to meet Pepys, who records in his diary several conversations which he had with him, — one was at a dinner given by the brethren of the Trinity House, and another at Pepys's own office.[17] Such a career would have left an ordinary man little time for literary work. And yet, as I have said in my history, he was always writing. We may adopt a phrase which Bagehot applied to Brougham, and say that, "for many years he rushed among the details of his age and wrote as he ran." It is reckoned that the number of his books and pamphlets exceed two hundred. Most of them are fugitive controversial pieces. But there are many serious books on all sorts of subjects, religious and political; and during his tenure of office as keeper of the

[17] *Diary* (Wheatley's Ed.), ii, 244, v, 279.

records, he published valuable works, illustrated by records up to that time unprinted. Among them we may note his Register of Parliamentary writs, an Abridgment of the Records in the Tower of London said to have been collected by Cotton,[18] and the Animadversions on Coke's *Fourth Institute*. But, before he became keeper of the records, and indeed throughout his life, he was a conscientious seeker after truth. He always honestly tried to base his historical work on the best evidence. This is clear from such works as the "*Demurrer to the Jews' long-discontinued Remitters into England*," and his "*Plea for the House of Lords*." Sir Charles Firth says,[19] "In point of style Prynne's historical works possess no merits . . . the arrangement . . . is equally careless. Yet, in spite of these deficiencies, the amount of historical material they contain, and the number of records printed for the first time in his pages, give his historical writings a lasting value." He urged upon the common lawyers the need to study the continental literature of commercial law, if they were to make the best use of the opportunity which their victory over the court of Admiralty had given to them; and he had visions of making, and inducing Parliament to enact, a revised edition of the statute law."[20]

[18] But the better opinion is that the collection was made by William and Robert Bowyer, see *D.N.B.*, Cotton, p. 313.

[19] *D.N.B.*

[20] *Pepys's Diary* (Ed. Wheatley), v. 279 — he "did discourse with me a good while . . . about the laws of England, telling me the many faults in them; and among others, their obscurity through multitude of long statutes, which he is about to abstract out of all of a sort; and as he lives, and Parliaments come, get them put into laws, and the other statutes repealed, and then it will be a short work to know the law, which appears a very noble good thing."

In the latter part of the seventeenth century Dugdale (1605–1686) is an outstanding figure.[21] Dugdale had been intended by his father for a lawyer, but he preferred historical research. He attracted the notice of Henry Spelman, who helped to get him a post at the Herald's College. There he prospered, and became Garter-King at Arms. His largest works — the *Antiquities of Warwickshire,* and the *Monasticon* — are historical rather than legal. But the writing of both these works had involved the acquisition of much information upon certain topics of legal history. Friends persuaded him to publish these notes; and the two works in which they appear are the *Origines Juridicales* and the *Chronica Series.* "The *Origines Juridicales* gives us in somewhat scattered form, some information about the origins of English law and English legal institutions, and a catalogue of law writers and law books. The book is chiefly valuable for the information which it gives us as to the history of the legal profession and of the Inns of Court. Dugdale tells us much of the forms and ceremonies of the legal life of the past and of his own day — of the creation of serjeants; of the origins, officers, social customs, educational and disciplinary arrangements, of the Inns of Court and Chancery; of the manner in which the Inns were controlled by the judges and the government. Till the publication by the Inns of Court of their records in the latter half of the last century, his book was the chief authority for the history of the Inns; and it is by no means superseded even at the present day. The *Chronica Series* is a chronological table of the chancellors, treasurers, judges, law of-

[21] Holdsworth, *H.E.L.*, vi, 595–597.

ficers and the king's serjeants from the Conquest till his own day. It is constructed from the records to which reference is always made; and the references are usually correct. It is a very valuable piece of work which, for all time, will be useful to legal historians." [22]

The eighteenth century gave us Thomas Madox [23] — one of the greatest of our English historians — whose works on very many aspects of legal institutions, it is safe to say, will never lose their value to many different kinds of historians. Madox was born in 1666. He became a student of the Middle Temple, but was never called to the bar. He chose an official career. He was clerk, first in the Treasurer's remembrance office, and then in the augmentation office. Finally, in 1714, he succeeded Thomas Rymer as historiographer royal to Anne and George I. He died in 1727. His works in order of date are: (1) The *Formulare Anglicanum,* which was published in 1702. It is a most valuable collection of mediaeval charters, which is indispensable to historians of mediaeval conveyancing. (2) His greatest work — *The History and Antiquities of the Exchequer of the Kings of England,* which was published in 1711. One of the Appendices to this work contained the first printed text of the *Dialogus de Scaccario.* The book is of the first importance to all legal historians. Finance then as now touches many sides of national life, and is intimately allied to many branches of law. Similarly, the machinery of taxation and account was and is intimately allied to many of the institutions of law and government. Hence the

[22] Holdsworth, *H.E.L.*, vi, 596–597.

[23] See Professor Haseltine's two papers in *L.Q.R.*, xxxii, 265, 352, on which this sketch is based.

book, to use Professor Hazeltine's words, " serves a double purpose: it is the history of constitutional institutions and it is also an apparatus towards the history of the ancient common law." [24] (3) The *Firma Burgi* which was published in 1722. It is an essay upon the cities, towns and boroughs of England taken from the records. (4) His last work was the *Baronia Anglica,* which was published posthumously in 1736. It is, as its sub-title tells us, " an history of land-honours and baronies, and of tenure *in capite,* verified by records."

Madox had all the necessary qualifications of an historian — a competent knowledge of Anglo-Saxon, mediaeval Latin, and French, a competent knowledge of law, and a thorough knowledge of palaeography and diplomatic. Moreover he had what was even more important — a high ideal of the function of the historian — " in truth," he said, " writing of history is in some sort a religious act. It imports solemnity and sacredness: and ought to be undertaken with purity and rectitude of mind." [25] Desire for truth and reverence for the past inspired him to research long and deeply into the records. The ninety-four volumes of his transcripts in the British Museum attest the thoroughness of his work. And he was no mere antiquarian — he studied antiquities because he saw that, without that study, there could be no understanding of later periods of history. " The knowledge of antiquities is a part of the historical learning, and cannot be impugned without impugning History itself." [26] " 'Tis of some consequence to know and consider the ancient law,

[24] *L.Q.R.* xxxii. 286.
[25] *History of the Exchequer,* Epistle to Lord Somers, p. iii.
[26] *Ibid.,* viii.

to the end we may be better guided in judging, what things are proper to be received, and what to be rejected, when offers are made (if they chance to be so) at any important alterations therein. For when we discern what things are agreeable and what not, to the nature and genius of the law, and the constitutional polity of this realm; we shall be (if I am not mistaken) the better able to see and take care, that under colour of improving the fabric, we do not superstruct what will not well cement, or trench too deep in the foundation." [27]

His work was based on records, because they were evidence "of the highest nature." [28] But he was also well versed in the texts of the mediaeval chronicles, in the mediaeval law books, and in the work of his contemporaries [29] — he can correct even Littleton.[30] In doing this work, he was continuing the critical work on the sources of our law which Selden had begun, the work which it has been the special function of our modern school of historical lawyers to continue. It is not surprising that the work of such a man should have been very permanent, and that modern historians should have united to praise him. Maitland said of his history of the Exchequer that it was one of the greatest historical works of the eighteenth century; and of the *Firma Burgi* that "no one is likely to make much of a contribution to British municipal history who does not know and admire his Madox." [31]

[27] *Formulare Anglicanum*, Preface, second §, viii.

[28] *L.Q.R.*, xxxii. 353–354.

[29] *Ibid.*, 352–353.

[30] *Firma Burgi*, 2; *Baronia Anglica*, 215–227; both passages are cited *L.Q.R.*, xxxii, 367–368.

[31] *Collected Papers*, ii, 223.

(3) Writers on the history of legal doctrine

Madox's ambition was to write ' A History of the Ancient and Primitive law of England '. As Professor Hazeltine has said,[32] " we fail to grasp the full intent of our antiquary, if we do not observe that he was working towards that ultimate end, if we do not see that he viewed his historical treatises upon special topics as but parts of a larger whole — the history of the earlier constitution and law of England." Hence we get a good deal of information as to the history of legal doctrine in his books. There is much learning as to writs, there are side lights on ecclesiastical law and local customs, there is something in the *Firma Burgi* on so modern a subject as the theory of corporations; and, as I have already pointed out, there is much in the *Formulare Anglicanum* on the law and practice of mediaeval conveyancing.

Of other writers who have dealt with the history of legal doctrines, Somner's work on gavelkind is important.[33] Lambard had published a version of the Kentish Customs in his Perambulation of Kent; and had given a short account of some of the points mentioned in the custumal. Somner's aim was to give a fuller account both of the name ' gavelkind,' and the thing. At one point he goes beyond his subject, and gives us an interesting historical disquisition on an important point in the law of succession to chattels. Of considerably greater importance is the work of Henry Spelman (1564–1641).[34] He was a student of Lincoln's Inn,

32 *L.Q.R.*, xxxii, 285.
33 Holdsworth, *H.E.L.*, v, 404.
34 *Ibid.*, 401–402, 404.

but was never a professional lawyer. His chief work was done in the sphere of ecclesiastical history; but both his Glossary, and his tract on tenure by knight service, are works of first rate importance in our legal history. The Glossary was our earliest dictionary of legal and historical terms constructed on sound principles;[35] and both the title on 'Feuds' in the dictionary, and the tract on tenure by knight service, had a large influence on the future literature of the land law. Maitland has said,[36]

> "Now were an examiner to ask who introduced the feudal system into England? one very good answer, if properly explained, would be Henry Spelman, and if there followed the question what was the feudal system? a good answer to that would be an early essay in comparative jurisprudence. Spelman reading continental books saw that English law, for all its insularity, was a member of a great European family, a family between all the members of which there are strong family likenesses. This was for Englishmen a grand and a striking discovery; much that had seemed quite arbitrary in their old laws, now seemed explicable. They learned of feudal law as of a medieval *jus gentium*, a system common to all the nations of the West. The new learning was propagated among English lawyers by Sir Martin Wright; it was popularized and made orthodox by Blackstone in his easy attractive manner. Now this was an important step — this connecting of English with foreign law, this endeavour to find some general intelligible principles running through the terrible tangle of our old books. Most undoubtedly there was much in our old law which could be explained only by reference to ideas which had found a completer development beyond seas, and to Blackstone and to Wright, and above all to Spelman, we owe a heavy debt."

[35] For an account of some of these early law dictionaries see an article by J. D. Cowley in the *Juridical Review*, xxxvi, 165–170.

[36] *Constitutional History*, 142.

(4) The collectors of original documents

We have seen that Madox based his works on the records, from which he printed many extracts, that he printed the text of the *Dialogus de Scaccario,* and that he published a collection of charters in his *Formulare Anglicanum.* But the first large collection of documents was Rymer's *Foedera.* Rymer was born in 1641 and died in 1713. His early literary efforts were in the realm of the drama and dramatic criticism. But, by the year 1684, he had definitely turned to the study of constitutional history. He was made historiographer royal in 1692; and, when Lord Somers persuaded the government to print a collection of treaties in 1693, Rymer was put in charge of the undertaking. He took as his model Leibnitz's *Codex Juris Gentium Diplomaticus.* In spite of difficulties in getting reimbursed for the large sums which he spent on the work, he printed fifteen volumes between 1704 and 1713; and five more volumes were printed by his co-editor Sanderson between 1715 and 1735. The documents range from 1101 to 1654. The work was received with enthusiasm both in England and abroad. A later edition of the first seventeen volumes was issued between 1727 and 1730; and a further edition in ten volumes, which contains new documents, was issued between 1735 and 1745. Another even more important collection for the legal historian was the *Rolls of Parliament,* the publication of which was taken in hand in 1765 by order of the House of Lords. This work, though defective, if measured by modern standards of historical scholarship, has done good service to the study both of legal and of constitutional history. We shall see that the publication of original documents in the nineteenth century, both by the government and by many learned societies, has been one of the main causes of the advancement of the study of English history in general, and of the study of legal history in particular.

But I must now turn from these border-line historians to four writers whose work places them definitely in the category of legal historians. We shall see that they were all influenced by the work of some of these groups of historians whose achievements I have summarized.

The Legal Historians

Two of the four historians of whose work I intend to speak come from the seventeenth century. They are Selden and Hale. Two come from the eighteenth century. They are Blackstone and Reeves.

Selden.[37]

Selden was born in 1584. He was educated at Oxford and the Inner Temple, and was made a bencher of that society in 1633. He entered Parliament in 1623. He took an active part in the impeachment of Buckingham in 1626; and in 1627 was counsel for Edmund Hampden, who had been committed to prison for refusing to lend money to the king. He was one of the members committed to prison in 1629, after the dissolution of the Parliament which had passed the Petition of Right. In the Long Parliament he was a moderate member of the constitutional party. He opposed

[37] *D.N.B.*; Life prefixed to Wilkins's Ed. of his works; C. W. Johnson, *Memoirs of Selden*; two articles by Professor Hazeltine, *H.L.R.*, xxiv, 105, 205.

the attainder of Strafford; and at one time the king thought of making him chancellor. When the war broke out he adhered to the side of the Parliament, but took no very active part in public affairs. Till his death in 1654 he devoted himself mainly to his literary work.

Selden was a man of immense and varied learning — in Milton's words [38] "the chief of learned men reputed in this land." Besides his works on legal history, he wrote much on questions of international law, English history, political and constitutional, ecclesiastical history, and classical and oriental subjects. It is with his works on legal history that we are here concerned. They comprise the following works: (1) The *Dissertatio ad Fletam*, a new edition and translation of which has just been published by Mr Ogg, who has prefixed to it an interesting and luminous introduction.[39] The Dissertation gives us an account of some of the earlier writers on English law, and of aspects of English legal history from the earliest times to Edward I's reign. The question to which most attention is paid is the question of the extent of the influence of Roman law on the development of English law.[40] (2) Notes upon Fortescue's *De Laudibus*, and on Hengham's *Magna and Parva*, which show Selden's mastery of mediaeval law. (3) Two tracts on the origins of the law as to probate, and as to the administration of and intestate succession to chattels, which Maitland thought were the best authorities on these two questions.[41] (4) Some

[38] *Areopagitica.*

[39] *Cambridge Studies in English Legal History.*

[40] For Selden's serious mistake as to the identity of Vacarius see *ibid.*, Introduction, xxvii–xxix.

[41] P. and M., ii, 330, 354 (1st Ed.).

short tracts on matters of constitutional interest — the Office of the Lord Chancellor, the Privileges of the Baronage, and Legal Judicature in Parliament.

I think that Selden can be regarded as the first scientific historian of English law. For the first time a first rate scholar and historian, who was also a first rate lawyer, applied his talents to the criticism of the sources and rules of English law. No other man of that day possessed the same range of knowledge, and hardly any other showed such industry. And this knowledge and industry were applied in accordance with the exacting tests of modern scholarship. His work was based on original documents, which were made to tell their tale with as little intrusion as possible of the author's personality. In addition, he possessed two qualities which made his work as legal historian particularly effective. In the first place, he was no mere antiquarian. His experience as a practising lawyer and a member of the House of Commons taught him to avoid what he called the " sterile part of antiquity,"[42] and to act upon the sound principle that history is useful only in so far as it "gives necessary light to the present."[43] In the second place, he was learned in other systems of law besides the common law. This enabled him to compare the rules and principles of English law with those of foreign systems at parallel stages in their development; and, as Maitland rightly said, there can be no effective legal history without such comparison.

Selden's literary style is often crabbed, and the arrange-

[42] Preface to the *History of Tithes*.

[43] Dedication to the *History of Tithes*, cited *H.L.R.*, xxiv, 112.

ment of his subject matter is sometimes faulty. But his great intellectual qualities justify us in regarding him both as the pioneer of the select band of English legal historians, and one of the most eminent of its representatives. No more appropriate name than Selden's could have been found for the Society, which, in our own days, has done so much for the cause of legal history.

Hale[44]

Hale was born in 1609. He was the friend and executor of Selden; and it was Selden, so Burnet tells us, who "first set Mr Hale on a more enlarged pursuit of learning, which he had before confined to his own profession." Hale was a student of Roman law and English history, a student of natural science, philosophy and religion, and a great collector of manuscripts and records, as his collection which he bequeathed to Lincoln's Inn Library shows. He soon made a name for himself at the bar. He advised Strafford, Laud and others accused by the Long Parliament; and it is said that he advised Charles I to plead to the jurisdiction of the High Court of Justice which was set up to try him. In 1649 he took the engagement to be faithful to the Commonwealth, and was made a judge of the Common Pleas in 1654. He refused to take a new commission from Richard Cromwell, and was active in forwarding the Restoration. After the Restoration he was made Chief Baron of the Exchequer. In 1671 he was made Chief Justice of the King's Bench. In 1676 failing health compelled him to retire. He

[44] Burnet, *Life and Death of Sir Mathew Hale;* Holdsworth, *H.E.L.*, vi, 574–595; *D.N.B.*

died at the end of the same year — regretted both by king and people.

Hale was the greatest English lawyer who had appeared since Coke. He had learnt to study law in Selden's school; and the lessons which he had there learnt made him what Coke never was, a legal historian. As an historian of English law he must be accounted Selden's superior, because, whilst Selden devoted only a small part of his time and talents to English legal history, this was Hale's chief study. His books show that as a legal historian he was equalled by no English lawyer before Maitland.

The four books upon which his fame as a legal historian rests are (1) *The History of the Common Law;* (2) *The Jurisdiction of the Lords' House;* (3) a tract on certain aspects of the royal prerogative connected with the revenue; (4) *The History of the Pleas of the Crown.*

Hale's *History of the Common Law* — the first history of the common law as a whole — is a rough sketch which was published after the author's death. It is fragmentary; and there is only a very meagre account of the history of legal doctrine. But, in spite of its fragmentary character, it has considerable merits. There is a clear statement of some of the leading characteristics of the common law; a wide acquaintance is shown both with the professional and historical literature; and, at appropriate places, comparisons are made with Norman and foreign laws. The important epochs and tendencies are duly stressed. Moreover the scantiness of the history in its later periods is supplemented by Hale's Preface to Rolle's *Abridgment,* in which an account is given of more recent changes in the law.

The Jurisdiction of the Lords' House, which was published by Hargrave in 1796, is a complete book, but was not finally revised by the author. Hale had written much on this subject from the early days of the Long Parliament. This essay, which was written after the Restoration, represents his final judgment on the matter. Considering that many of the questions discussed were some of the most controversial questions of that day, the judicial impartiality with which the book is written is a striking testimony to Hale's qualities as a scientific historian; and the fact that many of his views on these controversial questions have prevailed is a testimony to his statesman-like qualities.

Similar qualities are seen in his tract, in three parts, on the rights of the crown and private persons to rivers and the foreshore, on sea ports, and on customs duties. Throughout this tract Hale's mastery of records, and knowledge of the practice of the Exchequer practice, are remarkable.

The History of the Pleas of the Crown is, from the practising lawyer's point of view, the most important of his works. It is unfinished. Only the first out of the three projected books was completed; but it was left in a more perfect state than any of his other books. It was ordered by the House of Commons to be printed in 1680, but it was not published till 1736. The subject was one which could not be stated intelligibly without an historical treatment. Hale gives us a complete statement of the principles and evolution of the law. It was at once accepted, and has ever since been regarded as a legal classic.

Hale's first hand knowledge of legal and constitutional history enabled him to attain an impartiality impossible to most lawyers of the age of the Great Rebellion and the Restoration. The post-Revolution lawyers were apt to assume that the views of public law, which the Revolution had caused to prevail, were necessarily historically true. This was by no means the case. But it is not till almost our own days that a more scientific study of history has demonstrated this truth, and, by demonstrating it, has enabled us to appreciate Hale's real greatness as a legal historian.

I pass now to the two historians of the eighteenth century.

Blackstone[45]

Blackstone was born in 1723. He was educated at Charterhouse and Pembroke College, Oxford. In 1747 he was elected a fellow of All Souls, and was called to the bar in 1746. He did valuable work for the college by the manner in which he introduced order into its finances, and completed and arranged the Codrington library; and he did equally valuable work for the University Press. Murray, the solicitor-general — the future Lord Mansfield — tried to get him appointed regius professor of civil law; but the Duke of Newcastle gave the post to another — probably because he was dissatisfied with Blackstone's political views. This was a fortunate event. Murray persuaded Blackstone to break new ground by giving lectures on English law at Oxford. These lectures were the foundation of the *Commentaries,* and led to his appointment as first Vinerian Professor, when that chair was established in 1758, in accordance

[45] *D.N.B.;* Foss, *Judges,* viii, 243; Dicey's article on the Commentaries, *National Review,* liv, 653; Holdsworth, *L.Q.R.,* xxxix, 23–28; *Sources and Literature of English Law,* 155–161.

with the terms of Viner's will. The *Commentaries* were published in 1765, and at once made their author famous. He was a member of the House of Commons 1768–1770. In 1770 he became a judge of the Common Pleas.[46] He died in 1780.

He was a good judge; but I think that it is too much to say, as Foss says, that he was as distinguished as a judge as he was as a commentator. It is upon his *Commentaries* that his fame, both in England and America, rests. Of the merits of the *Commentaries*, and of the great effects which they had on the future history of the law, and on the teaching and literature of the law, I do not intend to speak. Blackstone's greatest successor, the late Professor Dicey, has delivered a final judgment upon these matters in his valedictory lecture.[47] I intend to speak of Blackstone only in one capacity — in his capacity of legal historian.

The *Commentaries* were not avowedly a book upon legal history. They were a statement of the law of Blackstone's own day. But the law of Blackstone's day could not be stated intelligibly without large historical explanations. It is for this reason that the *Commentaries* had, as I explained in my last lecture, a large influence in implanting in the legal profession a sound tradition as to the historical development of the law. But, though the *Commentaries* were not avowedly a legal history, they were in fact the best legal history of the common law as a whole up to Black-

[46] For a few months he changed places with Yates, J., and became a judge of the King's Bench, but he returned to the Common Pleas on Yates's death a few months later, see Foss, *Judges*, viii, 249.

[47] *National Review*, liv, 653.

stone's own time. And, at the present day, they can be regarded as not only a legal history, but also an historical document of great value for the legal history, not only of the eighteenth century, but also for many preceding centuries.

In his inaugural lecture, which was prefixed to the *Commentaries,* Blackstone emphasized the need for the study of legal history. He proposed, he said,[48] to trace the elementary principles of law to their origins — "to the customs of the Britons and Germans, as recorded by Caesar and Tacitus; to the codes of the northern nations on the continent; and more especially to those of our own Saxon princes; to the rules of the Roman law either left here in the days of Papinian, or imported by Vacarius and his followers; but above all, to that inexhaustible reservoir of legal antiquities and learning, the feudal law, or, as Spelman has entitled it, the law of nations in our western orb." He performed what he promised. All through the book legal principles are explained by reference to their history; and he concludes his *Commentaries* by giving, in the last chapter of the fourth volume, an historical summary of the chief epochs in the history of English law. The reasons why he thus treated law historically were mainly two. In the first place, he realized that its principles would not be rationally taught except in this way. In the second place, he recognised that the study of the principles of the law on historical lines was a condition precedent to well considered reforms. Of this latter reason I must say a word or two.

It has sometimes been said that Blackstone praised indiscriminately all things established. That was the favourite

[48] *Comm.,* i, 35–36.

gibe of Bentham and his school. And there is an element of truth in it. One glaring instance is his justification of the law as to benefit of clergy as it stood in his day.[49] But it is less true than is sometimes thought. Thus, he criticizes that part of the poor law which relates to the law of settlement;[50] he suggests changes in the law of inheritance;[51] he does not approve of the manner in which the king was compensated for the abolition of the incidents of tenure by the grant of an hereditary excise;[52] he criticizes the doctrine that a felon's blood was corrupted and the consequences which were deduced from it;[53] he does not approve of the Game Laws, — a "bastard slip" of the forest law — which, he aptly said, "have raised a little Nimrod in every manor;"[54] he criticized the conflicting character of the rules of law and equity;[55] and he favoured the project of a general register of deeds and wills.[56] One of the reasons, which he advanced in his inaugural lecture for an academic study of the law, was the fact that professors of the law might "suggest expedients . . . for improving its method, retrenching its superfluities, and reconciling the little contrarieties, which the practice of many centuries will necessarily create in any human system."[57] I think that the

[49] *Comm.*, iv, 371.
[50] *Ibid.*, i, 365.
[51] *Ibid.*, ii, 233.
[52] *Ibid.*, ii, 77.
[53] *Ibid.*, ii, 256.
[54] *Ibid.*, iv, 416 — "the forest laws established only one mighty hunter throughout the land, the game laws have raised a little Nimrod in every manor."
[55] *Comm.*, iii, 441.
[56] *Ibid.*, ii, 342–343.
[57] *Comm.*, i, 30.

Commentaries as a whole show that Blackstone kept this reason in his mind, and that he illustrated its truth. No doubt he, like other eighteenth century lawyers and statesmen, had a prejudice in favour of things established. But it was a reasoned prejudice based on historical grounds. It was no fanatical prejudice, and it enabled him, as it enabled Maitland,[58] to suggest sane reforms in the law.

For these reasons I claim that Blackstone was a legal historian; and, since his *Commentaries* cover the whole field of English law, I claim that he was the only historian of English law as a whole who had yet appeared. And, if we ask what were the intellectual qualities which made him so successful a legal historian, I think the answer is somewhat as follows:

In the first place he was a master of the literature of both law and history. If we look at the authorities which he cites, we can see that he was well acquainted with all the English authorities legal and historical, with the texts of Roman law, with foreign commentaries on Roman law, with writers on international law and jurisprudence, with the work of political thinkers such as Locke, Montesquieu, and Beccaria. In one respect it might perhaps be contended that he in some measure anticipated the need for the practice, adopted by the modern editors of the Year Books, of collating the records with the Year Book — a practice which Maitland regarded as an important advance in the study of English history; for, speaking of reports, he says " these serve as indexes to, and also to explain the records; which

[58] See Maitland's Paper on the Law of Real Property, *Collected Papers*, i, 162.

always in matters of nicety and consequence the judges direct to be searched."[59]

In the second place, his wide reading taught him the two truths which Maitland has emphasized — first that history involves comparison, and secondly that effective legal history is the history of ideas. The following passage from his inaugural lecture shows that he had grasped these two truths: the "primary rules and fundamental principles [of English law] should be weighed and compared with the precepts of the law of nature, and the practice of other countries; [they] should be explained by reasons, illustrated by examples, and confirmed by undoubted authorities; their history should be deduced, their changes and revolutions observed, and it should be shown how far they are connected with, or have at any time been affected by, the civil transactions of the kingdom."[60] All through the four volumes of the *Commentaries* Blackstone introduces comparisons with foreign law, and tries to get down to the fundamental ideas which underlie the legal rules in force at different periods in the history of English law.

In the third place, the attractiveness of his style, which even Bentham admitted, and the supreme literary tact which Dicey has emphasized, enabled him to produce a book which was literature. Indeed, it is difficult to estimate the debt which law and legal history owe to the literary style of Blackstone and Maitland. Both these great teachers have made many students by the charm of their style.

The success of Blackstone as a legal historian is, I think, undoubted. It is no doubt true that many parts of his

[59] *Comm.*, i, 71. [60] *Comm.*, i, 36.

historical work have not stood the test of modern research and criticism. On the Anglo-Saxon period he is weak — he is too ready to accept the conclusions of those seventeenth century lawyers and historians who had used Anglo-Saxon history for political purposes. His views as to the connection of uses with the Roman *fideicommissum* are clearly wrong; and, probably because he was influenced by Lord Mansfield's views as to moral obligation, he has no idea of the true origin of the doctrine of consideration. But from the reign of Edward I onwards, his history is generally sound and valuable. Pollock and Maitland's great history covers the period during which Blackstone's work is weakest. That history and the *Commentaries* present a picture of the historical development of English law down to Blackstone's own date, which, in its main outlines, is very fairly adequate.

Blackstone had not set out to write legal history; but he was a legal historian. We must now turn to a writer who deliberately set out to write a complete history of English law, but who had far less success as a legal historian than Blackstone.

John Reeves [61]

Reeves was born in 1752 or 1753. He was educated at Eton and Oxford, and became a fellow of Queen's College. He was called to the bar in 1779. From 1791–1792 he acted as chief justice in Newfoundland. Afterwards he held various official appointments, and was made king's printer in 1800. He was a classical scholar, had some knowledge of

[61] *D.N.B.*

Hebrew, and was a fellow of the Royal Society and of the Society of Antiquaries. He died in 1829. He was a strong Tory, and founded an association "for preserving liberty and property against levellers and republicans." His strong political views led to the most remarkable episode in his career — his prosecution, by order of the House of Commons, for publishing a pamphlet in which he magnified the power of the king, and maintained that Parliament and Juries were mere adjuncts of the Constitution.[62] The attorney-general, Sir John Scott — the future Lord Eldon — prosecuted. It was a libel of a very opposite kind to those which he was usually employed to prosecute at that time; and he must have agreed with a good deal in the pamphlet. In fact he did not press the case very hard against the accused, who was acquitted.[63]

Reeves wrote many books and pamphlets; but we are only here concerned with his *History of English Law.* The first volume was published in 1783, the second in 1784, and a second edition, with a continuation to the reign of Philip and Mary, in 1787. A third edition was published in 1814, and a further continuation to the end of Elizabeth's reign in 1829. A new edition, edited by Finlason, was published in 1869.

The history was the first complete history of English law,

[62] (1796) 26 *S.T.*, 530.

[63] The jury said that the pamphlet was an "improper publication," but that as there was no seditious intent they found him not guilty. It was said that this censure was occasioned by one obstinate jury-man who refused to acquit unless the jury would insert it; the other eleven were in favour of an immediate acquittal, 26 *S.T.*, 594–595.

for the period which it covered, which had ever been written. It was inspired, so the author tells us, by the closing chapter of Blackstone's *Commentaries* — he aspired, he said, "to fill up with some minuteness the outline there drawn."[64] The book is not without merits. The author gives a careful account of the history of procedure and pleading. He had sufficient historical sense to be rightly sceptical as to the authority of the Mirror of Justices.[65] He alludes to the point, recently taken by Mr. Bolland, that the words of the statute De Donis Conditionalibus are not wholly consonant with the interpretation which the courts had put upon it.[66] But, it must be confessed that the defects outweigh the merits. First, the book is indescribably dull — indeed its dullness has probably injured the cause of legal history as much as the literary style of Blackstone and Maitland has helped it forward. Secondly, it is written from purely legal sources. Thirdly, the author has no sense of proportion, and no idea that the "sterile part of antiquity" ought to be avoided. He describes the most minute technicalities at inordinate length. Fourthly, there is no attempt to connect the history of law and legal ideas with the political, social or economic ideas of the day — indeed Reeves, differing from Blackstone, expressly denies that legal history should be written in this way.[67] The only ideas which he

[64] Preface to 1st Ed.

[65] Vol. ii, 232–238.

[66] Vol. ii, 200; *cp.* Holdsworth, *H.E.L.* (3rd Ed.), iii, 114–116.

[67] "It has been apprehended that much light might be thrown on our statutes by the civil history of the times in which they were made; but it will be found on enquiry that those expectations are rarely satisfied," Preface to 1st Ed.

discusses are the technical ideas of the common law. These, coupled with bald narratives of events, summaries of statutes, and a slight account of the literature of the law at different periods, make up the book.

The book has suffered badly at the hands of Finlason, its latest editor. Finlason was a learned but muddle headed lawyer with no historical sense. Reeves had passed somewhat lightly over the Saxon period — being more at home with the law from the period of Glanvil onwards. Finlason had some very exaggerated ideas as to the continuance of the influence of Roman law from the time of the occupation of the Romans; and he believed that the Mirror of Justices gave a trustworthy account of the Saxon period.[68] Reeves was rightly sceptical as to the Saxon origin of the jury: Finlason had no doubt that the Saxons had a complete system of trial by jury, and could see little difference between trial by jury and trial by compurgation.[69] Unfortunately for Reeves, his book is usually read in Finlason's edition incumbered by Finlason's notes.

" Unreadable and unread " has been the description applied to Reeves's book. Uninteresting it may be; but that it is not unreadable and has not been unread is plain from the fact that it has passed through several editions. In fact it has had its uses as a book of reference. It gives us an intelligent abstract of many old authorities, and useful information on the history of writs, procedure, and pleading.

The time when the book appeared was not a time favourable to the historical study of the law. The best intellects were turning to Bentham and that rationalistic utilitarian

[68] Preface to 1st Ed. note (a). [69] Vol. i, 37, note (a).

school, of which I gave some account in my last lecture. It was not till the revival of historical studies in the nineteenth and twentieth centuries that men's minds began to turn again to the historical study of the law. Of the rise of this new school of legal historians I shall speak in my next lecture.

III

FOUR OXFORD PROFESSORS

In this lecture I propose to give, in the first place, some account of the influences which made for the revival of the study of legal history in the latter half of the nineteenth century, and of the results of that revival. In the second place, I propose to say something of the four Oxford Professors — Maine, Vinogradoff, Dicey, and Sir Frederick Pollock — whose work entitles them to be reckoned as some of the most eminent representatives of this new historical school.

The Historical Revival and its Results

John Stuart Mill, in his two consecutive essays on Bentham and Coleridge,[1] has given pointed expression to the contrast between the rationalistic and utilitarian school of *a priori* thinkers about law, and the new historical school. Bentham was the representative of the first of these schools, which, as we have seen, was antagonistic to history. Coleridge was the philosophical representative of the second of these schools. He and his followers did not try to test beliefs or institutions by narrow *a priori* tests of their own devising, and condemn all that could not satisfy those tests. Rather, as Mill says, they considered that "the very fact that any doctrine had been believed by thoughtful men, and

[1] *Dissertations and Discussions*, i, 330, 393.

received by whole nations and generations of mankind, was part of the problem to be solved, was one of the phenomena to be accounted for."[2] They held that "the long or extensive prevalence of any opinion was a presumption that it was not altogether a fallacy."[3] Hence, "the brilliant light which has been thrown upon history during the last half century, has proceeded almost wholly from this school."[4]

Ever since Mill wrote, the movement in favour of an historical revival has been growing, not only in force, but also in intelligence. What were the causes of this revival, the beginnings of which Mill witnessed and welcomed, the triumph of which was to prove the narrowness of the philosophy of which his father had been so eminent an exponent? I think that it may be said that there were two main causes. First, this revival was a result of the great political upheaval of the French Revolution, and the many other upheavals which followed after. Secondly, it was one of the results of the great scientific discoveries of the nineteenth century.

(1) The French rationalistic philosophers, who applied to morals and law and legal institutions a criticism of the same *a priori* kind as that which Bentham applied to English law and legal institutions, helped to shape the course of the French Revolution. But, as Vinogradoff has said,[5] "the disillusionment brought about by the excesses of the French Revolution obscured for a time the historical significance of the upheaval, and brought discredit on the cult of reason as

[2] *Dissertations and Discussions*, i, 394.
[3] *Ibid.*
[4] *Ibid.*, 426. [5] *Historical Jurisprudence*, i, 124.

preached by the Terrorists." This reaction took many forms; but all these forms tended to revive interest in the old institutions, the old beliefs, the old customs, which the rationalistic school had condemned, and had attempted to abolish. It was a revival of national feeling which was the decisive factor in the final defeat of Napoleon; and this revival of national feeling led to the growth of interest in the nation's past. That interest took not only a literary form, as in Walter Scott's novels; not only a political form, as in Burke's denunciation of the ideas behind the French Revolution; but also the form of a revival of historical and comparative studies in many branches of knowledge — in language, in folklore, in ethnology, and in religion. As Vinogradoff has pointed out,[6] Jacob Grimm was a scientific student, not only of the German language, but of Germanic mythology and popular law.

In the realm of law the reaction first took definite shape in the rise of the historical school which is associated with the name of Savigny. Thibaut, a well known professor of law at Göttingen, had proposed to codify the law of the German states, taking as his model Roman law and the French civil code. Savigny protested, on the ground that the law of a nation was as dependent on its history as its language or its religion; and that therefore a code ought to reflect the history of a nation's law, and embody those national characteristics which were the product of its history.[7] This new historical school introduced a new way of regarding law. As Vinogradoff has said, "Instead of being

[6] *Encyclopædia Britannica*, Art. "Historical Jurisprudence."
[7] *Historical Jurisprudence*, i, 128.

traced to the deliberate will of the legislator, its formation was assigned to the gradual working of customs. . . . As regards the State, law was assumed to be an antecedent condition, and a consequence of its activity. In this way direct legislation was thrust into the background, while customary law was studied with particular interest, and regarded as the genuine manifestation of popular consciousness."[8] The strength of this new historical school was shown at the end of the century in the conflicts over the enactment of the German civil code, which ultimately came into force January 1, 1900. The first commission, headed by Windscheid, had produced a code in which the influence of Roman law was marked. Its production caused a strong protest from the historical school. Gierke proved that there was much in the code which was contrary to the principles of Germanic law. "The general result was," as Maitland has said, "unfavourable to the draft [code]. It was condemned as too abstract, pedantic, doctrinaire, too Roman, and too un-German." This was remedied by the work of a second commission, which produced the draft which was eventually enacted. The result showed the strength of the historical school, and was a personal triumph for Gierke.[9]

(2) The progress of this historical school was enormously helped by the change in the character of scientific speculation as to all matters affecting organic life, which was the necessary result of the Darwinian theory of evolution. As I said in my first lecture, the rationalistic school, consider-

[8] *Ibid.*, 129.

[9] Vinogradoff, *Historical Jurisprudence*, i, 131-132; Maitland, *Collected Papers*, iii, 474-488.

ing only those branches of science which were concerned with inanimate nature, had tried to discover laws which were as universally true of human activities as the laws which governed inanimate nature. But this was impossible. As Sir Leslie Stephen has said,[10] "The importance of taking into account the genetic point of view, of inquiring into the growth as well as the actual constitution of things, is obvious in all the sciences which are concerned with organic life. Though we cannot analyse the organism into its ultimate constituent factors, we can learn something by tracing its development from simpler forms. This method is applicable to biology as well as sociology. Some theory of evolution was required in every direction." The Darwinian theory gave a new scientific backing to the upholders of the historical school, because, to use Dean Pound's terminology, it substituted a biological for a mechanical interpretation of the facts of life.[11] It reinforced the central theory of that school, that the law of any nation is dependent on its history; and that, consequently, there could be no proper understanding of a nation's law without a study of its history.

These two causes tended to turn men's minds away from the rationalistic and purely analytical manner of regarding law, and to turn their minds to the view that the right understanding of the present state of the law, and consequently, intelligent suggestions for its reform, were not possible without a knowledge of its history. It is due to these two causes that throughout Europe and America, during the last

[10] *The English Utilitarians*, iii, 374.
[11] *Interpretations of Legal History*, 72.

seventy or eighty years, the importance of all kinds of historical studies has been realised and magnified. It is due to them that the study of Anglo-American legal history has been not only revived, but also reformed, and brought up to the standard demanded by the new tests of accuracy which have come with the scientific study of history.

It is probably true to say that in England the conflict between the two schools was not so bitter as it was abroad. I have already pointed out that, even in the heyday of the influence of Bentham and his school, the professional tradition of the historical development of the law influenced the reforms which were made under Bentham's influence. Similarly, the first forty years of the nineteenth century saw the publication of much historical work which has a very direct bearing on legal history.

In the first place, important books had begun to appear. Hallam's *Middle Ages* was published in 1818, and his *Constitutional History* in 1827. Palgrave, who did much for the publication of the Public Records generally, and the records of Parliament in particular, published his *English Commonwealth* in 1832, and his essay upon the Council in 1834. Spence, between 1846 and 1849, published his two volumes on the history of the equitable jurisdiction of the court of Chancery — a pioneer work which sheds much light on many parts of our legal history, and is still of great use. In the second place, original documents were being printed both by the government, and by private societies. Of the work of the government I shall speak a little later. As to the private societies it is well to remember that both the Camden Society and the English Historical Society began to publish unpublished material in 1838; that the Roxburgh Club began to publish in 1814; and that the Surtees Society began to publish in 1835.

Much historical work was thus being done during the first half of the nineteenth century, but, if we compare the first half of the nineteenth century with the second, I think that it is clear that the influences which, throughout Europe, were making for the intensive study of history, and especially the influence of the Darwinian theory, enormously increased the importance attached to the historical point of view in all branches of learning, including law. Perhaps the best illustration of the manner in which in England the importance of the historical point of view gradually gained recognition, and affected the study of Anglo-American law, can be found in the history of the measures taken in the nineteenth century to preserve and publish the Public Records.[12]

In the year 1800 the condition of the Public Records was a scandal. In spite of intermittent enquiries and commissions in the eighteenth century, no efficient measures had been taken to house or preserve the records, and far less to calendar or index them. Since the regular places of deposit — the Chapter House at Westminster, the Exchequer Buildings, the Rolls chapel, and the Tower — were too small to contain them, they were housed in all sorts of unsuitable places; and, when deposited in these places, they were entirely neglected. Prynne, in Charles II's reign, described the records in the Tower as a confused chaos, buried under

[12] See Holdsworth, *H.E.L.* (3rd Ed.), ii, 599–602, and the references there cited.

corroding putrefying cobwebs, dirt, and filth in the dark corners of Caesar's chapel in the White Tower. To study the records (as he did) under these conditions was, as he rightly said, "heroic." They were in the same condition in 1800. In that year the Record Commission was established. That Commission lasted for thirty-seven years, and it did good work in printing and publishing many records — such publications as the Charter Patent and Close Rolls, the calendars of Chancery proceedings, the Placita Quo Warranto and the Hundred Rolls, the Placitorum Abbreviatio, and the Statutes, have been of enormous service to legal historians. But the Commission did little for the care and preservation of the records. "The report," says Maitland,[13] "that comes to us from the year 1833, from the office of the king's remembrancer, tells a hardly credible tale of wild disorder. There were sacks upon sacks of documents the general nature of which was utterly unknown to their custodians. Confusion had been confounded by removals. In 1822 the old Exchequer Buildings had been pulled down to make way for those new Law Courts which have now in their turn disappeared; some of the records were carried to the stone tower at the great gate of Westminster Hall, others were buried in a shed erected inside the hall, and, when, in 1830, a coronation demanded the suppression of this 'ark' as it was called, they were carted off to the king's mews at Charing Cross. It was said that the 'soldiers and common labourers' who effected the first of these transportations had shown their sense of the high value of certain documents by selling them to the manufacturers of glue."

[13] *Memoranda de Parliamento* (1305) (R. S.), xiii.

It was perhaps little wonder that the proceedings of the Record Commissioners aroused criticism. Moreover the editorial work of their publications was attacked. Charges of jobbery were made; and, amid the acrimonious discussions which ensued, the Commission went under. That meant that no more records were printed at the public expense.

The appointment of the Record Commission, and the fact that, during its life, much valuable material had been published, show that the Legislature was not wholly blind to the value of history, or to the necessity of basing history on original material. But we may perhaps regard the decision, after the breakdown of the Commission, to print no more records, as due in part to the fact that the importance of accurate history, based on the records, was as yet imperfectly realised. However that may be, the controversies over the Commission had one good result — they called attention to the condition of the records. A report of a committee of the House of Commons in 1836 had emphasized this aspect of the question. The result was the passing in 1838 of the Public Record Act[14] which established one Record Office, and made provision for its use by the public.

It is largely due to this Act, to the manner in which it was administered by two successive Masters of the Rolls, Lord Langdale and Lord Romilly, and to the other measures which they have taken, that, when the value of the study of history became more distinctly realised, the Public Records were fully and freely available to students.

[14] 1, 2 *Victoria*, c. 94.

Of Lord Langdale Foss has said that "he devoted himself with indefatigable industry to cleanse the Augean stable of the public records," and that he "justly gained for himself the title of the Father of Record Reform." [15] Foss's *Lives of the Judges*, a work of reference essential to all legal historians, which has done all and much more than all that Dugdale's *Origines Juridicales* and *Chronica Series* did for the seventeenth century, was perhaps the first book of legal history to profit by Lord Langdale's labours. The author bears witness to the fact that, as the result of these labours, the statesman, the historian, and the biographer had facilities which they had never before enjoyed; [16] and, in his dedication to Lord Langdale, he bears witness to the manner in which Lord Langdale's achievement had helped him in the composition of his book. But, in Lord Langdale's time, the new opportunities, which his policy had given to historical students, were not as yet fully realised. Gairdner tells us,[17] in the introduction to the *Paston Letters*, that the Record Office, when first constituted, "was supposed to exist for the sake of litigants who wanted copies of documents, rather than for that of historical students who wanted to read them with other objects. Besides, people did not generally imagine that past history could be re-written, except by able and graphic pens which, perhaps, could put new life into old facts without a large amount of additional research. . . . Even the States Papers were kept apart from the Public Records, and could only be consulted

[15] *Lives of the Judges*, ix, 144.
[16] *Lives of the Judges*, iii, 21.
[17] *The Paston Letters* (Ed. 1910), Introduction, xxix, xxx.

by special permission from a Secretary of State." It was Lord Langdale's successor, Lord Romilly, who not only revised the rules of the Record Office with the object of making its contents more easily accessible to historical students, but also induced the government in 1857 to start the Rolls Series.[18]

That series has done good work in publishing unprinted material, and in providing new critical editions of books already printed. It is true that not all of the publications in it are of equal merit.[19] When it was started the number of men fit to edit mediaeval MSS. was not large; and some few books in that series are really bad. Twiss's edition of Bracton is no improvement on the seventeenth century edition, which Selden pronounced to be full of errors; and there is a tale of an edition of Glanvil which was printed, but never published, because it was so incompetently edited. Such accidents happened in the early days of the series — accidents which we can regard the more complacently now that Professor Woodbine is giving us at last an adequate Bracton, and we hope also an adequate Glanvil. On the whole the Rolls Series has been of very great service to legal historians. Think, for instance, of the Black Book of the Admiralty, of the Red Book of the Exchequer, of the Munimenta Gildhallae, of the Ramsey Cartulary, and, above all, of the Year Books. The two editors of the Year Books in this Series — Horwood and Pike — for the first time applied modern critical methods to the MSS. of the Year Books, and thereby did a work which is an indispensable

18 Foss *Judges*, ix, 253–254.
19 Maitland, *Collected Papers*, iii, 499–500.

preliminary to the writing of the mediaeval history of English law.

I think that it may be said that the Rolls Series did two other great services to history in general, and to legal history in particular.

In the first place, it set an example of publishing original material which has been extensively followed. Societies, such as the Early English Text Society, the Pipe Roll Society, and a large number of local societies, have provided much raw material for many aspects of our history; and for legal history the foundation of the Selden Society in 1887 was the beginning of a new epoch. Maitland, its first literary director, both by his own writings and by his encouragement and inspiration, carried it over its initial difficulties, and set a standard of achievement which is surpassed by no other similar Society. Think of the volumes of early plea rolls, of the records of all sorts of local courts, of the records of the Star Chamber, Admiralty, the Chancery, and the court of Requests; its editions of texts — the text of the Mirror, and just recently Professor de Zulueta's text of Vacarius; Maitland's volume on Bracton and Azo; its Year Book series; the volume of Select Cases in the Law Merchant, and the volume of Select Cases before the King's Council — the mere enumeration of their titles is sufficient to show the large debt which all legal historians owe to this Society.

In the second place, the demand for editors, created in the first instance by the institution of the Rolls Series, and then by other Societies, has trained historians. Stubbs's Introduction to the series of chronicles, which he edited for the Rolls Series, was a preparation for his *Constitutional History* — a great contribution to the history of the public law of the Middle Ages. Pike, the editor of the Year Books, has given us the *History of Crime* and a *Constitutional History of the House of Lords*. Many of the Introductions to the Selden Society volumes — notably Mr. Turner's Introduction to the *Select Pleas of the Forest*, Mr. Marsden's Introduction to *Select Pleas of the Admiralty*, and Mr. Leadam's Introductions to *Select Pleas in the court of Requests and the court of Star Chamber* — are treatises on the subjects to which they relate.

The progress of the idea that law must be studied historically is, I think, most forcibly illustrated by Stephen's *History of the Criminal Law*. Stephen admired the school of analytical jurists; some of his most important work was done in the sphere of codification; and in his Digest of the law of evidence he tried to base the whole law of evidence upon the logical doctrine of relevancy. But as your two great writers on the law of evidence — Thayer and Wigmore — have shown, older ideas of procedure and pleading must be taken into account; so that the law, as it stands to-day, cannot be explained without a consideration of the historical causes, which have been the parents of rules, inexplicable solely by reference to this logical doctrine. But, in spite of this, Stephen was influenced by the historical tendencies of his day. In his review of Austin's and Maine's books[20] he admitted the barrenness of much of the discussion of the analytical jurists, and testified to the manner in which men's minds were turning to history. "History," he

[20] *Edinburgh Review*, cxiv, 456 (Oct., 1861).

said,[21] "has been consulted upon almost all the great standing subjects of human thought. Politics, morals, and theology have all been studied from this point of view, and Mr. Maine is now applying the same process to law." Like John Stuart Mill,[22] he regarded Austin's and Maine's speculations as the complements of each other;[23] and, it may be added, he acted on this belief; for his *History of the Criminal Law* is the complement to his Digest of that branch of the law.

When it appeared in 1883 it was probably the best modern history of a particular branch of English law that had yet appeared in England. It won high praise from Pollock and Maitland. English criminal law, they said,[24] will be fortunate in its historians, "for it will fall into the hands of Matthew Hale and Fitzjames Stephen." Though the more intensive study of the earlier history of our law has rendered some parts of it obsolete, it is still the best history of the later stages of the law. And it has another merit which it can never lose. The fact that its author was a practising lawyer and a judge, gives to his account of many parts of the law, and especially to his analysis of famous trials, the reality and the vividness which comes of practical experience.

At this point I close my account of the historical revival and its results, and I proceed to deal with the four Oxford Professors who have some claims to be considered to be

21 *Ibid.*, 481.

22 *Essay on Austin,* "Dissertations and Discussions," iii, 211-212.

23 *Edinburgh Review,* cxiv, 481 —"History and analysis, so far from being inimical, are complementary to each other, and neither can be safely dispensed with."

24 P. and M., ii, 446 (1st Ed.).

(after Maitland) the most eminent representatives of this revival.

The Four Oxford Professors

Three of these professors — Maine, Sir Frederick Pollock, and Vinogradoff — were the holders of the Corpus Chair of Jurisprudence. One — Dicey — was the holder of the Vinerian chair. All except Sir Frederick Pollock have passed away. I shall speak first of Maine and Vinogradoff, because the character of their work, and the extent of their influence, have some affinities. I shall then speak of Dicey, and lastly of Sir Frederick Pollock.

Maine [25]

Maine was born in 1822. He was educated at Pembroke College, Cambridge, and attained great distinction as a classical scholar. As Sir Frederick Pollock has said,[26] "he entered the University an unknown young man; he left it marked as among the most brilliant scholars of his time." After taking his degree, he began to study law, became law tutor of Trinity Hall in 1845, and Regius Professor of civil law in 1847. Both as a law tutor and as professor he attained a marked success. In fact he had all the qualities of a good lecturer — a powerful voice, a style like crystal, and every sentence perfectly finished. He was called to the bar in 1850; and in 1852 he became the first Reader on Roman Law at the Inns of Court. From 1862–1869 he was legal

[25] *Life and Speeches of Sir Henry Maine*, by Whitley Stokes, with a memoir by Grant Duff; Pollock, *Oxford Essays*, 147-186; Vinogradoff, *The Teaching of Sir Henry Maine*, *L.Q.R.*, xx, 119–133.

[26] *Oxford Essays*, 149.

member of the Viceroy's council in India, and Vice Chancellor of Calcutta University. It was then that he got that knowledge of Indian law and institutions of which he made so great a use in his books. On his return in 1869 he was made first Corpus Professor of Jurisprudence at Oxford. In 1877 he became Master of Trinity Hall, and in 1887 Whewell Professor of International Law at Cambridge. He died in 1888.

Vinogradoff recognised Maine as " one of his most influential teachers," and testified to his European reputation — " the whole of my generation of students have had to deal directly or indirectly with the ideas propagated by him or similar to his." [27] As Vinogradoff points out, both the German historical school of Savigny, which, as we have seen, was a nationalist school and an opponent of the rationalists, and the Darwinian theory, influenced his intellectual point of view.[28] These two influences led him, on the one hand, to stress the importance of history to the proper understanding of legal and social development, and, on the other, to base his deductions on the best historical evidence. Thus he applied to jurisprudence those historical and comparative methods which in other domains, notably philology and anthropology, had already achieved remarkable results. Stephen truly said that he was " the first person who in this country had brought to such an attempt the special professional knowledge [of the law] which was indispensable to success in it." [29] And the brilliance of Maine's execution

[27] *L.Q.R.*, xx, 119.
[28] *Ibid.*, 125, 127.
[29] *Edinburgh Review*, cxiv, 481.

was equal to the novelty of his plan. His wide reading, his capacity for observation, and his intuitive capacity for seeing to the heart of a problem, enabled him to produce books which influenced the juridical thought of Europe and America.

It may perhaps be asked on what grounds I claim Maine as an historian of Anglo-American law. Was he not, it may be said, rather the founder of the school of Historical Jurisprudence in England? Was not his chief work done in the sphere of comparative law? Did not Roman law and Hindu law fill a larger place in it than English law? In answer to this objection I put in three pleas. My first plea is that the very fact that Maine was a student of comparative law made him better fitted than most English lawyers to be an effective historian of English law. My second plea is that in some of his essays he gives valuable sidelights on points of English legal history — on the origin of the manor in his *Village Communities;* on the origin of feudalism in his *Early Institutions;* on the position of the king in his essay on the relation of the king to early civil justice in *Early Law and Custom;* on the nature of equity in his analysis of the idea of Equity in *Ancient Law;* and on the nature of the influence of Bentham and his school in his pregnant remark, in the same book, that the theory of the *jus naturale* was, to the Roman lawyers, " the ancient counterpart of Benthamism." My third and strongest plea is that his claim to a place among the historians of our law rests upon the fact that his books taught, and still teach, students of law to think, and to think historically.

They teach all students of law to think. I myself read

the *Ancient Law* when I was at school; and I know of no book which gave me so many new ideas, which opened up so many vistas of thought. When, later, I read his other books I found that they were equally effective as sources of inspiration. And I go further and say that the more knowledge one has, and the more one reads them, the more one can get out of them. One may cease perhaps to agree with all Maine's views; but his books still inspire thought; and the thought which they inspire is historical. It is because the thought which they inspire is historical thought that Maine must be given a place amongst our legal historians. He, more than any other man, brought Englishmen round to the belief that law and legal institutions must be studied historically if they are to be understood. He thus added many recruits from the legal world to the forces which, as we have seen, were putting historical studies of all sorts on a new basis; and so helped to create that historical school of lawyers which, in the last half of the nineteenth century, has transformed the study of English law and English legal history.

As to the truth of this aspect of Maine's work I can vouch to warranty no less an authority than Sir Frederick Pollock. In his *Oxford Lectures* [30] he says: "We may at least say, looking to our own science of law, that the impulse given by Maine to its intelligent study in England and America can hardly be overrated. Within living memory the Common Law was treated merely as a dogmatic and technical system. Historical explanation, beyond the dates and facts which were manifestly necessary, were regarded

30 At pp. 158-159.

as at best an idle ornament, and all singularities and anomalies had to be taken as they stood, without any reason or (perhaps oftener) with a bad one. It was an unheard of process to show that they were really natural products in the development of legal conceptions. . . . A certain amount of awakening was no doubt effected by the analytical school. . . . But the analysis of modern political and legal ideas in their latest form could not lead to any rational explanation of an actual historical system. . . . The scientific study of legal phenomena, such as we really find them, had no place among us. . . . Maine not only showed that it was a possible study, but showed that it was not less interesting and fruitful than any in the whole range of the moral sciences. At one master stroke he forged a new and lasting bond between law, history, and anthropology. Jurisprudence itself has become a study of the living growth of human society through all its stages."

This, then, is the great and lasting contribution of Maine to the study of our legal history. And his contribution was made the more effective, even as Blackstone's and Maitland's were made the more effective, by the charm of his style — a charm which he owes to the fact that, as Sir Frederick Pollock has said, "he was a humanist before he was a jurist, and never ceased to be a humanist."[31] And so, although many of his conclusions are not now accepted, his books will always be studied, because they show the workings of the mind of a genius in the domain of legal history, because they have an artistic form which cause them to last long after more learned books have passed into oblivion.

[31] *Oxford Essays*, 150.

To quote Sir Frederick Pollock once more: "Maine can no more become obsolete through the industry and ingenuity of modern scholars than Montesquieu could be made obsolete by the Code Napoleon."[32]

Vinogradoff[33]

Vinogradoff was born in Russia at Kostroma in 1854. He had an hereditary connection with education, since he was the son of the director of schools at Moscow. He graduated at Moscow in 1875, and, after that, studied in Berlin in Mommsen's and Brunner's seminars, and in Italy. From 1884 to 1901 he held the chair of history at Moscow. While at Moscow he both laid the foundation of his encyclopaedic knowledge of law and history, and did good work, on the Moscow city council, for the cause of education in the great province of Moscow. The measures of the government, which seriously interfered with the intellectual activities of the students, and the freedom of the professors, led, in 1901, to Vinogradoff's resignation. He came to England, and in 1903 he began his twenty-two years tenure of the Corpus chair of Jurisprudence. In 1910 and 1911, at the request of his old colleagues, he gave some courses of lectures at Moscow as honorary professor. But in 1911 the government introduced police spies into his lectures. Consequently he,

[32] *Oxford Essays*, 154.

[33] Articles by Sir Bernard Pares, A. Meyendorff, and myself in the *Slavonic Review for 1926*; an article by Professor de Zulueta in *Law Quarterly Review*, xlii, 202; an article by Dr. Powicke in *English Historical Review*, xli, 276; the memoir which I have written for the British Academy. I have repeated in this lecture some parts of what I have written for the *Slavonic Review*, and in the memoir for the British Academy.

with some sixty professors and lecturers, resigned their posts. At the beginning of the war he worked for English and Russian solidarity; and it was not till after the Bolshevik revolution in 1917 that he gave up all hope of a normal constitutional development for Russia. In 1918 he became a British subject. After the war he steadily worked on; and, at the time of his death, he was gathering up the results of a long life of study into his great *Treatise on Historical Jurisprudence*, of which, unfortunately, he only lived to publish two volumes. He died in Paris in December, 1925.

Vinogradoff did a great work in the fields of legal history and historical jurisprudence. His relation to his great predecessor Maine, whom, as we have seen, he recognised as "one of his most influential teachers," may, I think, be stated in this way: Maine made a series of comprehensive surveys of many fields of jurisprudence: Vinogradoff carried on his work by the manner in which he accurately mapped and charted the ground which Maine had only surveyed. Maine formed the connecting link between Savigny's school of historical jurisprudence, and the modern historical school, of which Vinogradoff was one of the most eminent representatives.

Vinogradoff's work as an author falls roughly into two main divisions. First, there is the series of books and papers in which he has elucidated many of the problems of the origins and mediaeval development of English social and legal history. Secondly, there is the series of books on the theory of the law. It is with the first of these series that we are here concerned.

The first and in some ways the best of the longer books in this series is *Villainage in England,* which appeared in its English dress in 1892. It shed a wholly new light on the social and legal aspects of the institution of villainage; and it won high praise from Maitland. In the introduction Vinogradoff showed that power, which he was afterwards to show in his writings on legal theory, of summarizing the work of his predecessors, both English and foreign, and of thus bringing the work of English writers into relation with the work of continental writers. His next book — *The Growth of the Manor* — appeared in 1905. In the interval between 1892 and 1905 Pollock and Maitland's *History of English Law* had appeared; and much had been written on the manor and cognate subjects by Round and Seebohm. *The Growth of the Manor* co-ordinated the results of these researches, summed up their conclusions, indicated the problems which still awaited solution, and described the important position which the manor occupied in the mediaeval state. It was based on his lectures; and that it has proved to be one of the most valuable of this series of books to the student is shown by the fact that it has reached its third edition. *English Society in the Eleventh Century* (1908) attempted to analyse the various elements — Old English, Danish, and Norman — which made up English society in that century of rapid change. An examination is made of the influence of political factors and public law on social life; of the influence of economic factors, and their effect on husbandry and the rules of private law; and of the various classes and groups which were created by the working of these political and economic causes. It is not an easy book to read; and the trend of the argument is not always obvious. But, in spite of these defects, it is a most valuable historical analysis of the forces which were creating mediaeval society in England.

These three books were concerned as much with social as with legal history. Vinogradoff's work on the Year Books of Edward II in the Selden Society's Series was concerned mainly with legal history. It shows a mastery of the MSS. sources, and of the complications of the legal procedure of the fourteenth century. But Vinogradoff was more familiar with the law of England up to the early part of the fourteenth century, than with the later periods in its history; and, for this reason, he lacked the capacity to see, so readily as Maitland saw, the germs of doctrines which became important in later law.

All these books were concerned primarily with English history; but they could not have been written if Vinogradoff had not also possessed a wide knowledge of Roman law, ancient history, and European mediaeval history. His wide knowledge of all these great subjects is illustrated by his work on the origins of the mediaeval society of Western Europe in the *Cambridge Mediaeval History*. In the three chapters which he contributed to that history he has given us a luminous summary of the decay of the ancient and the growth of modern society throughout Western Europe — a summary which affords an indispensable background to the special studies of the historians of particular nations.

Vinogradoff wrote many shorter books and papers on subjects connected with the social and legal history of the Middle Ages. The following are some of the most important. In 1914 he, together with Mr. Frank Morgan, edited for the British Academy the *Survey of the Honour of Denbigh.* It is a most valuable document, because it presents us with a survey of a tract of country on the borders of England and Wales, which brings before us the clash and contrast of the Celtic tribal customs, and the more highly organized and the more individualistic English manorial system. Since the Celtic record sheds much light upon the ideas at the back of that element of tribal law, which is present both in Celtic and Germanic institutions and laws, this piece of work must be regarded as a necessary pendant to Vinogradoff's books on English social and legal history. In 1908, at the Berlin Historical Congress, he read a paper on *Reason and Conscience in Thirteenth-Century Jurisprudence,*[34] which for the first time indicated the position in the literature of English law of St. Germain's *Doctor and Student,* and its importance in the history of equity. In 1909 he published his little book on *Roman Law in Mediaeval Europe,* which is the only up-to-date English authority on a topic, some knowledge of which is essential to the student of all sides of mediaeval life and thought. With this book may be mentioned his paper in 1923 on the *Roman Elements in Bracton's Treatise.*[35] In 1913, in his Creighton Lecture on *Constitutional History and the Year Books,*[36] he showed how much light the Year Books can be made to shed both on the position of the common law in the constitution, and on concrete problems of mediaeval constitutional law.

[34] *Law Quarterly Review,* xxiv, 373.
[35] *Yale Law Review.*
[36] *Law Quarterly Review,* xxix, 273.

In 1918 he contributed a paper to the Magna Carta Commemoration Essays. In 1923 he wrote a most suggestive paper on the use and position of maxims in the early common law [37] — a paper which suggests some useful comparisons with the much later use of maxims in the creation of our system of equity. But perhaps the two most striking of his shorter papers are his essay on Folkland in the *English Historical Review* for 1893, and his paper in the *Athenaeum* on 19 July, 1884, in which he describes his rediscovery of the MS. which has come to be known as Bracton's Note Book.

In his paper on Folkland Vinogradoff disposed of Allen's theory that folkland was *ager publicus,* and restored the interpretation of Spelman, who had held, in the seventeenth century, that it was land held by individuals according to the folk or customary law. This restoration of Spelman's view necessitated a considerable revision of existing theories of Anglo-Saxon law and society, and it got rid of a good many of the difficulties which Allen's interpretation had caused. Vinogradoff's discovery of Bracton's Note Book restored to the world of historical scholarship a MS. which had been lost to sight since Fitzherbert used it in the composition of his Grand Abridgement. It also set Maitland to work on his first great book — his edition of the Note Book — in which he proved the correctness of Vinogradoff's conjecture as to its origin, and produced an introduction on the law in Bracton's day which is one of the most brilliant essays which he ever wrote. With this paper on Bracton's Note Book we must put Vinogradoff's essay on the *Text of Bracton,* which he contributed in 1885 to the first volume of

[37] *Revue hist. de droit française et étranger* (4th Series), ii, 334.

the *Law Quarterly Review.* Maitland's verdict was that Vinogradoff "had learned in a few weeks more about Bracton's text than any Englishman has known since Selden died."

Vinogradoff's influence upon the study of legal history was not confined to his books. It rests also upon the works of the pupils whom he trained in his seminar. When he came to Oxford the seminar was an institution as yet unknown. He set to work to acclimatize this foreign institution. Helped by the foundation of the Maitland library, he got it started, and proceeded to educate in research a band of students who owned him as their master. The nature of his inspiration, and his eye for choosing his students, are proved by the eight volumes of *Oxford Studies in Social and Legal History.* It would be impossible to enumerate here all the papers which have appeared in that series. All are based on original work on MS. sources, and all have added to our knowledge of social and legal history. Such studies as Professor de Zulueta's on *De Patrociniis Vicorum,*[38] as Mr. Barbour's on the *History of Contract in Early English Equity,*[39] as Miss Cam's on *The Hundred Rolls,*[40] as Miss Putnam's on the *Early Treatises on the Justices of the Peace,*[41] as Dr. Jacob's on the *Period of Baronial Reform and Rebellion, 1258–1267,*[42] are works which do credit alike to the Professor who inspired them, and to his pupils who executed them.

Vinogradoff's work in the last years of his life was saddened by mental distress and physical difficulty. The course

[38] Vol. i.
[39] Vol. iv.
[40] Vol. vi.
[41] Vol. vii.
[42] Vol. viii.

of the Russian revolution destroyed long cherished hopes; and his eyesight was failing. But with a quiet heroism, which is not wholly unparalleled among scholars, he worked on at his *Historical Jurisprudence* and with his seminar. He has not worked on in vain. The work which he has done, or has inspired others to do, in these last years, has added materially to his fame. He leaves behind him at Oxford and elsewhere many scholars who are proud to have been his pupils, by whom he will never be forgotten. And his achievement, both as an author and as a teacher of authors, will be more permanent than these memories. He will long be remembered as the Professor who performed the difficult task of adding to the reputation of a Chair which had been held by Maine and Pollock; as the Professor who gave to a law school, adorned by such English lawyers as Blackstone and Dicey, a reputation for cosmopolitan learning, which has spread its fame in lands which do not own the sway of English law.

Both Maine and Vinogradoff were professors of jurisprudence, and were as distinguished for their knowledge of comparative law as for their historical learning. I pass now to a lawyer who was more distinctively an English lawyer, and an English legal historian.

Dicey [43]

Dicey was born in 1835. He was an undergraduate at Balliol, a fellow of Trinity, and won the Arnold Prize with his earliest historical work — an essay on the Privy Council.

[43] See Holland's article in *L.Q.R.*, xxxviii, 276.

He was called to the bar, and became counsel to the Inland Revenue in 1876. In 1882 he returned to Oxford as Vinerian Professor of English law — an office which he held till his resignation in 1909. He died April 7, 1922.

Dicey was the first holder of the Vinerian chair after it had been reconstituted and further endowed by All Souls College. I think that it can be safely said that Blackstone, the first holder of the chair on the old foundation, and Dicey its first holder on the new, have united to give this chair a prestige which is not surpassed by that of any other chair of English law. In fact, these two professors will take a very similar place in our legal literature. Dicey will hold, in the history of the legal literature of the nineteenth century, a place not unlike that which Blackstone holds in the legal literature of the eighteenth century; for both have written books which became classics whilst they were still alive.

The two books which give Dicey his place as a legal historian are his books on the *Law of the Constitution*, and his *Law and Opinion in England*.

No one can write a good book on English constitutional law without a knowledge of legal history. Dicey's book is a classic, because he added to his knowledge of English law a knowledge both of the constitutional law of other states, and a knowledge of English history. I do not think that English students, before Dicey's book was published, had any adequate knowledge, either of what continental administrative law was, or of what was involved in that rule of law, which followed upon the refusal of the English people to countenance anything like a system of administrative law; and I do not think that they had realized that, but for the abolition of the Star Chamber in 1641, England might well have had a system of administrative law. Similarly, he was the first lawyer to explain the relations of those conventions of the constitution, upon which the system of cabinet government rests, to the law of the constitution.

Dicey's book on *Law and Opinion in England,* which had its origin in a course of lectures delivered at Harvard on the history of English law, is at once a work of genius, and a model to legal historians. Dicey takes three great currents of opinion — the old Toryism (1800–1830), Benthamism or Individualism (1825–1870), and Collectivism (1860–1900), — and shows how they have influenced the course of legislation during the nineteenth century. At the same time he takes account of (1) the " counter or cross currents," which have caused legislation to differ from what it would have been, if the dominant tendency of the time had won an undisputed victory; and (2) the effect of case law on legislation. The effects of what was perhaps the most important of these cross currents — the effect of ecclesiastical considerations — is carefully worked out; and his account of the effect of the combined efforts of the judges of the courts of common law and equity upon the proprietary status of married women, is the best existing historical account of this branch of the law. I said in a preceding lecture that Pollock and Maitland's *History of English Law,* combined with Blackstone's *Commentaries,* present a picture of the historical development of English law down to Blackstone's time, which is very fairly adequate. If we add to these books the first edition of Dicey's Law and Opinion we get an adequate history of its development down to 1900; and if we add the introduction to the second edition we carry the history as far as 1914.

I pass now to the only survivor of these eminent representatives of the historical school — Sir Frederick Pollock.

Sir Frederick Pollock

Sir Frederick Pollock is not only the oldest and the most eminent of living English legal historians, but also he has some claims to be considered the most eminent of living English lawyers. I do not think that any other lawyer is at once so learned in English law, and so learned in comparative law and jurisprudence. At the same time, I know of no other living lawyer whose technical books have so much literary flavour. What he said of Maine is even more true of himself — "he was a humanist before he was a jurist, and he has never ceased to be a humanist."

It is unnecessary to go through the long list of Sir Frederick Pollock's books and essays. They are known to all Anglo-American lawyers. But I think we may say this of them: whether he is explaining modern English law, as in his books on contract and tort; whether he is explaining the fundamental conceptions underlying bodies of law in general, or underlying particular branches of the law, as in his *First Book on Jurisprudence*, or in his *Essays in Jurisprudence and Ethics;* or whether he is explaining the history of developments in the common law as a whole, or in some particular branch of that law, as in his *Expansion of the Common Law*, his *Genius of the Common Law*, or his essay of the King's Peace — we see that power of stating difficult technical doctrines clearly and simply, which is the touchstone of the master, and that felicity of expression which is the mark of a man of letters. I suppose that all of you have read his *Leading Cases Done into English* — if not, do so at once. And from his other books and notes in the *Law Quarterly Review* an anthology of good things could be culled. I will content myself with citing two examples: In his little book on the Land Law he says, "to be lord of a manor is to be the lord of a secular ruin, in which he that knows the secret of the crabbed spell book may call up ghosts of a vanished order of the world."[44] The statute of Uses and its results have never been so picturesquely described as in the following passage from the *Expansion of the Common Law:*[45] "The arbitrary legislation of the Tudor period plunged us into a turbid ocean, vexed by battles of worse than fabulous monsters, in whose depth the gleams of a *scintilla juris* may throw a darkling light on the gambols of executory limitations, a brood of coiling slippery creatures abhorred of the pure Common Law, or on the death struggle of a legal estate sucked dry in the octopus-like arms of a resulting use; while on the surface a shoal of equitable remainders may be seen skimming the waves in flight from that insatiable enemy of their kind, an outstanding term."

It is because Sir Frederick Pollock has so thoroughly absorbed the spirit of our law, it is because he is able to express that spirit so felicitously, that he has disclosed in his own writings the secret of the success of the common

[44] *The Land Law*, 11.
[45] *The Expansion of the Common Law*, 13.

law — the secret of being able to impart to its students a sense of the sanctity of the law and of the high nature of the lawyers' calling. That sense finds its first expression in Bracton, and has always been part of the creed of the great lawyers who have come after him. I shall close this lecture by giving you some portions of a passage, which not only shows Sir Frederick's style at his best, but also is the most eloquent exposition of the creed of all true common lawyers.[46] Sir Frederick Pollock is giving advice from the Corpus Chair to students of the law; and I think that no passage in English literature (except it may be some passages from Burke) shows more clearly the reverence for law which is created by that mastery of it which can come only from its historical study:

" And what is to be the reward of your labours when you have brought all your best faculties to bear on your chosen study. . . . The reward which I promise you is this, that your professional training, instead of impoverishing and narrowing your interests, will have widened and enriched them; that your professional ambition will be a noble and not a mean one; that you will have a vocation and not a drudgery; that your life will be not less but more human. Instead of becoming more and more enslaved to routine, you will find in your profession an increasing and expanding circle of contact with scholarship, with history, with the natural sciences, with philosophy, and with the spirit if not with the matter of the fine arts. . . . As a painter rests on the deep and luminous air of Turner, or the perfect detail of a drawing of Leonardo; . . . such joy may you find in the

[46] *Oxford Essays*, 108–111.

lucid exposition of broad legal principles, or in the conduct of a finely reasoned argument on their application to a disputed point. And so shall you enter into the fellowship of the masters and sages of our craft, and be free of that ideal world which our greatest living painter has conceived and realised in his masterwork. I speak not of things invisible or in the fashion of a dream; for Mr. Watts in his fresco that looks down on the Hall of Lincoln's Inn, has both seen them and made them visible to others. In that world Moses and Manu sit enthroned side by side, guiding the dawning sense of judgment and righteousness in the two master races of the earth; Solon and Scaevola and Ulpian walk as familiar friends with Blackstone and Kent, with Holt and Marshall; and the bigotry of a Justinian and the crimes of a Bonaparte are forgotten, because at their bidding the rough places of the ways of justice were made plain. There you shall see in very truth how the spark, fostered in our own land by Glanvill and Bracton, waxed into a clear flame under the care of Brian and Choke, Littleton and Fortescue, was tended by Coke and Hale, and was made a light to shine round the world by Holt and Mansfield, and the Scotts, and others whom living men remember. You shall understand how great an heritage is the law of England, whereof we and our brethren across the ocean are partakers, and you shall deem treaties and covenants a feeble bond in comparison of it; and you shall know with certain assurance that, however arduous has been your pilgrimage, the achievement is a full answer. So venerable, so majestic, is this living temple of justice, this immemorial and yet freshly growing fabric of the Common Law, that the least of us is happy who hereafter may point to so much as one stone thereof, and say, The work of my hands is there."

I have as yet said nothing of that one of Pollock's works which will perhaps live longer than any of them — the great *History of English Law* of which he and Maitland were the joint authors. But, as the preface indicates, that book is more Maitland's than Pollock's, and so for that reason I shall speak of it in my last lecture, which will deal with Maitland and his achievement. There is also another reason for adopting this course. That history is a great book because more than merely English authorities went to the making of it. It owes something both to American and to foreign lawyers and historians. We cannot therefore properly appreciate it till something has been said of the American and the foreign contribution to our legal history. Of these two matters I shall speak in my next lecture.

IV

THE AMERICAN AND FOREIGN CONTRIBUTIONS

THE American contributions to the study of Anglo-American legal history has been very large, and far more directly important than the foreign contribution. To know the history of the rules of our common law is obviously as important to American as to English lawyers; and Americans, like the rest of the world, have been influenced by that revival of historical studies of which I spoke in my last lecture. But that revival of historical studies has shown us that, though our law is the peculiar property of English speaking peoples; though it differs fundamentally at many points from the law of those countries which have developed their law from the basis of the technical conceptions of the Roman civil and canon laws; yet, to understand its development, we must take account of the influence of the Roman civil and canon laws at many different periods. That revival has shown us also that to understand its salient characteristics, we must be able to contrast its institutions and rules with those which were developed by other states in Western Europe. In this lecture, therefore, I shall deal first with the American, and secondly with the foreign contributions to the history of Anglo-American law.

The American Contribution

I do not intend to speak of the historians of purely American law — I am not competent to do so; and purely American law has not yet got its historian. Some day perhaps the story will be told either by an individual, or, as is more probable, by a group of individuals; for, though the story is short as compared with the story of Anglo-American law, the difficulty is great, since it is the story of the law of a federation of forty-eight states. That it can be done, and that it will be done some day, I do not doubt; and that it will be of enormous importance to all students of the common law, and to all students of comparative law, is obvious. In fact one small part of that story — the part which relates to the history of the legal profession, and to legal education — has been told in a most interesting manner by Mr. Warren in his *History of the American Bar*. In this lecture I intend to speak of the American contribution to the history of Anglo-American law.

Legal history owes a large debt to America. Look, for instance, at the series of *Essays on Anglo-American Legal History*, which were published by a committee of the Association of American Law Schools 1907–1909. In that series of seventy-six essays there are thirty-nine by American writers. These thirty-nine essays cover a vast range of subjects — the American colonial period, nineteenth century reforms in the law, the legal profession, legal education, the sources of law, the history of courts, procedure and pleading, evidence, equity, commercial law, contract, torts, property, testamentary and intestate succession. Moreover it must be remembered that this series of essays was but a small selection of the published work done by Americans on Anglo-American legal history; and that since 1909 very much more has been published both in books and in periodical literature.

It is obvious that, in the time at my disposal, I cannot hope to give a complete account of this large contribution to the history of our law. All I can do is to give, first, a short survey of the ground covered by some of your most distinguished authors; and, secondly, an estimate of the characteristics of the work which they have done.

(1) *A survey of the ground covered*

I think that it is true to say that the part of the ground which has been most completely covered is the large field of the *Common Law.* I shall therefore deal with this topic first. I shall then say something of the history of the law of *Real Property,* of the history of *Equity,* and of the history of *Legal Institutions.* Then I shall say something of certain *General Surveys* of important aspects or periods of legal development; and, lastly, I shall speak of the work done on the *Sources of the Law.*

The Common Law

The history of many parts of the law of contract and tort; the history of a part of the common law, closely allied in its earlier history to the law of tort, the law as to the possession and ownership of chattels; the history of commercial law; the history of the law of evidence; and the history of procedure — have all been put on a new basis by the writings of American lawyers. In these diverse fields of law I think the outstanding names are Bigelow, Holmes, Ames, Thayer, Wigmore, and Street. I propose to say something of the work of these authors, and then to mention more briefly one or two other contributors to the many topics which can be included under the general head of the common law.

Mr. Justice Holmes holds, I think, in some respects, the same place with you as Sir Frederick Pollock does with us. Both are great lawyers, great juridical thinkers, and men of letters, as well as legal historians. Holmes is also one of the greatest judges of a Court in which there have been many great judges. His book on *The Common Law* is one of the earliest, if not quite the earliest, of the histories of the principles of liability civil and criminal, of contract, of bailment, of possession and ownership, of successions after death and *inter vivos;* and he was the first to point out the Germanic origin of the law as to uses and trusts. Just as Selden warned historians against the "sterile part of antiquity," so he has warned us against "the pitfall of antiquarianism." [1] He has practiced what he has preached; for it was his historical researches into the history of the possession of chattels which played a large part in inducing the court of Appeal in England, in the case of *The Winkfield,*[2] to accept the correct historical view of the position of the bailee, and, by so doing, to give its sanction to all the implications of the common law theory of possession. His book on *The Common Law* was published in 1881; and it is remarkable how well most of Holmes's opinions on points of legal history have stood the test of time during the ensuing period of active historical research.

Bigelow, like Holmes, was one of your veteran historians — perhaps the earliest of your historical pioneers. His books have done much to elucidate the earliest period in the

[1] *Collected Legal Papers,* 194. [2] [1902] P. 42.

history of the law. The *Placita Anglo-Normanica*, published in 1879, contains a most useful selection of cases taken from the chroniclers, which range from 1066 to the first half of Richard I's reign. His *History of Procedure in England*, published in 1880, to which the author regarded his *Placita Anglo-Normanica* as an introduction, deals with the Saxon and Norman period.[3] It is still a most useful book. His able paper on the rise of the English will is included in the *Essays in Anglo-American Legal History*.

Ames's historical works on many branches of common law show that, if he had devoted all his talents to the field of legal history, he could have written a great legal history. He has illuminated the spheres of contract and tort, of ownership and possession, of uses and trusts. Perhaps his two greatest pieces of work were the papers in which he demonstrated that the origin of the doctrine of consideration, as applied to the law of contract, and the form which it has assumed, must be looked for in the history of the action of assumpsit;[4] and his discovery of the true relation of *Tyrrel's Case* to the doctrine that there could be no use upon a use, and to the later equitable modification of that doctrine.[5] In the introduction to the letters between Ames and Maitland, which the Cambridge Law Journal has recently published, Professor Hazeltine has told us that, when he showed to Maitland the list of essays, which it was pro-

[3] In the Appendix to this book there is a useful collection of Norman writs and charters relating to the eleventh and twelfth centuries, which are, as the author says in his preface, "the complement of the collection in the *Placita Anglo-Normanica*."

[4] *Lectures on Legal History*, 129–166.

[5] *Ibid.*, 243.

posed to publish in the *Essays in Anglo-American Legal History,* " Maitland scanned it carefully for several minutes and then remarked: 'Ames's essays are the best of the lot.' "[6]

Thayer's great book, the *Preliminary Treatise on the Law of Evidence,* was described, when it first appeared, as " a book which goes to the root of the subject more thoroughly than any text book in existence."[7] That was a true description; and it was a true description because Thayer was the first to treat the development of this branch of the law historically. He saw that the rules of the law of evidence cannot be treated, as Stephen treated them, simply as applications of the logical doctrine of relevancy. "The law of evidence," he said, " is the creature of experience rather than logic, and we cannot escape the necessity of tracing that experience."[8] In fact the law of evidence is a part of the law of procedure, and its rules have necessarily been affected by the many influences which, in the course of its long history, have affected that branch of the law. Now the common law procedure, like the common law system of pleading, is dominated by the existence of the jury; and the jury has been influenced by the older modes of trial which the jury superseded, and the old conception of a trial into which the jury system was born. Thayer's book gave us at length an entirely adequate history of the jury, and of those older modes of trial.

Wigmore is famous as a legal historian in the sphere of

[6] *Cambridge Law Journal,* ii, 1.
[7] Cited by Ames, *Lectures on Legal History,* 464.
[8] *Preliminary Treatise,* 267–268.

tort, but more especially in the sphere of evidence. His essay on the history of the Responsibility for Tortious Acts[9] gives us a complete account of this chapter of legal history, from its origins in early Germanic law down to the nineteenth century. His great treatise on the law of evidence not only gives a complete account of the existing law in all your forty-eight jurisdictions, it not only gives an account of all the important English cases, it is also a most skilful and interesting history of the whole of this branch of the law. I have used the historical parts of the treatise; and, from my own experience, I can say this: but for Wigmore's book it would have taken me much longer to write the section which I have devoted to this topic, and the section, when written, would have been very inadequate.

Professor Street's book on the *Foundations of Legal Liability* was described by a reviewer in the *Law Quarterly Review* as "a work of considerable pretensions and unusual merit."[10] It is a remarkable historical study of the ideas at the back of delictual and contractual liability; and, as a necessary part of that history, of the law of those actions by the working of which the principles of that liability were ascertained. It is exhaustive without being tedious; it is original and suggestive; and it is based on a thorough understanding of the vast number of decisions in which the law is contained. His accounts of contracts in general and of consideration, of bailment, and of negotiable instruments from the seventeenth century onwards, are particularly good.

[9] *Essays in Anglo-American Legal History*, iii, 474–537.
[10] *L.Q.R.*, xxiii, 228.

To enumerate all the other good work which has been done by many writers on different branches of the common law would be a long task. I can only mention a few, which are but samples of a large bulk; and I think that the bulk will be found to be fully up to the samples. There are a group of essays on Mercantile law — Burdick's essay on *Contributions of the Law Merchant to the Common Law,*[11] Cranch's essay on the history of promissory notes,[12] Vance's *History of Insurance Law,*[13] Beale's *History of the Carrier's Liability,*[14] Williston's *History of Business Corporations*[15] and Baldwin's *History of Private Corporations,*[16] Dr. Gross's volume in the Selden Society's publications on *Select Cases Concerning the Law Merchant.* In the sphere of contract and tort there is Hening's essay on *The Beneficiary's Action in Assumpsit,*[17] Veeder's *History of Defamation,*[18] and Bordwell's suggestive papers on property in chattels.[19]

I pass now from the topic of common law in general to the topic of real property.

Real Property

Some of Ames's essays bear indirectly on the history of this topic — his essay on the disseisin of chattels,[20] and on the nature of ownership;[21] and some of his other essays bear directly on it — his essays on injuries to realty,[22] on

[11] *Essays in Anglo-American Legal History,* iii, 34.
[12] *Ibid.*, 72.
[13] *Ibid.*, 98.
[14] *Ibid.*, 148.
[15] *Ibid.*, 195.
[16] *Ibid.*, 236.
[17] *Ibid.*, 339.
[18] *Ibid.*, 446.
[19] *H.L.R.*, xxix, 374, 501, 731.
[20] *Lectures on Legal History,* 172.
[21] *Ibid.*, 192.
[22] *Ibid.*, 219.

the origin of uses,[23] and the origin of trusts.[24] There is also included in the *Essays on Anglo-American Legal History* a good historical account of the action of ejectment by Sedgwick and Wait, from part of a treatise by the authors on the trial of title to land.[25] This is a topic which it is essential to understand if the history of this branch of the law, from the late sixteenth century onwards, is to be mastered. A chapter in the mediaeval land law is illustrated by Dr. Hemmeon's book on *Burgage Tenure in Mediaeval England.* But, as you all know, the most considerable American contribution to this branch of the law is to be found in the works of John Chipman Gray. His two books on *Restraints on Alienation* and the *Rule against Perpetuities,* and more especially the latter, were recognised at once as books of authority both in England and America. I think that it would be true to say that, with the possible exception of Judge Story, no book has been so frequently cited in an English court as Gray's *Perpetuities.* "Indeed," says Mr. Roland Gray,[26] "an English specialist on these topics, who differs from Professor Gray on many points, has feelingly complained that the tendency of our judges is to regard him as orthodox if not infallible"; and Mr. Roland Gray tells us that the book on *Perpetuities* "has been cited as authority in reported cases over the English speaking world from Manitoba to New South Wales and New Zealand."[27] Gray was a great lawyer, a great teacher, and, as his book on the *Nature and*

[23] *Ibid.*, 233.
[24] *Lectures on Legal History,* 243.
[25] Vol. iii, 611.
[26] *Memoir of John Chipman Gray* (1917), 33.
[27] *Ibid.*

Sources of Law shows, a great legal philosopher. I am sure that the authoritative character of his books is largely due to the fact that they contain, not only a complete statement of the law, but a complete history of the process by which that present state was reached. The student can see the rule, and the reason for the rule; and that enables him to decide to what states of fact the rule should be applied, and to what states of fact it is inapplicable. These two books are perhaps the finest examples in our legal literature of the use of applied legal history.

I pass now to the closely related topic of equity.

Equity

Two of the most striking discoveries in the history of equity are due to American lawyers. Holmes was the first to point to Germanic law for the true origin of uses.[28] Ames was the first to point out that the equity did not, immediately after the decision in *Tyrrel's Case*, enforce the use upon a use as a trust; and that that development did not take place till about a century later.[29] Holmes's view got rid of the idea that the origin of the use was to be looked for in Roman law; and its correctness has been reinforced by Maitland's researches. At the same time Ames pointed out, correctly enough, that, though the origin of uses must be looked for in Germanic law, though uses were well enough known before the establishment of the equitable jurisdiction of the Chancellor, it was by reason of their development in that jurisdiction that they acquired the form which they

[28] *Essays in Anglo-American Legal History*, ii, 705.
[29] *Ibid.*, 737.

ultimately took in our modern law. An essay worthy to be ranked with these essays of Holmes and Ames (and I can give it no higher praise) is Barbour's essay on the *History of Contract in Early English Equity,* which was published in Vinogradoff's series of *Essays in Social and Legal History.*[30] If Barbour's career had not been cut off by a premature death, I am sure that he would have made a great contribution to legal history. The manner in which he dealt with the mass of original material on his subject, not only enabled him to attain important results in that subject, but also indicated the manner in which other researchers into the early history of equity should deal with this mass of material.

Another book which has been of the greatest service to legal historians is Langdell's book on *Equity Pleading,* which was published in 1877. The historical sections of that book, which are printed in the *Essays in Anglo-American Legal History,*[31] show very clearly the debt of equity pleading to the civil and canon law, and explain equally clearly the contrast between the conceptions underlying the systems of equity and common law pleading. The acquisition of clear ideas on this matter is an indispensable preliminary to any history of this topic, because the later system of equity pleading owed something to both these systems of pleading; and it is only by looking at the manner in which they influenced one another, and at the gradually shifting relations of the elements derived from both these systems, that we can understand the system which was eventually produced, and can estimate both its good and its bad points.

[30] Vol. iv.

[31] Vol. ii, 753.

Two other contributions to the history of equitable doctrines have been made by Dean Pound. To the *Wigmore Celebration Legal Essays* he contributed a valuable account of consideration in Equity, which both recalls the fact, too often forgotten, that consideration is not a purely common law doctrine; and illustrates the very different treatment which the conception of consideration received in the court of Chancery.[32] To the *Cambridge Legal Essays* he has contributed a paper on *Certain Maxims of Equity*.[33] This is a much more important subject in the history of equity than in the history of the common law. As Maitland pointed out,[34] equity was never "a single consistent system, an articulate body of laws. It is a collection of Appendixes between which there is no very close connexion." I think that it is for this reason that the earlier writers on equity tended to group their account of the law round these maxims or principles; and, even to-day, as I have found by experience, it is possible to give a very fair account of the leading principles of equity on this plan.

I pass now to the topic of Legal Institutions.

Legal Institutions

Much has been done by American writers, both lawyers and laymen, to elucidate the history of our legal institutions. George Burton Adams has done most valuable work on the early English constitutional history, both in scattered essays in the *Columbia Law Review* and elsewhere, and in his *Origin of the English Constitution*. The history of the High Court of Parliament, and many topics in mediaeval constitu-

[32] At pp. 435–460. [33] At pp. 259–277. [34] *Equity*, 19.

tional history, have been illuminated by Professor McIlwain's interesting and inspiring books and essays. Professor Haskins's book on Norman institutions is essential to the right understanding of the influence of the Conquest on English institutions and English law. Miss Putnam has shed a flood of light on the working of the Statutes of Labourers — a subject which is at the root of a great deal of later law on the subject of employer and workman. In the sphere of local government there is Dr. Gross's volume in the Selden Society's publications on the Coroner's Rolls; Dr. Beard's essay on the Justices of the Peace; and Mr. William A. Morris's valuable work on the Frank-pledge system, and his recent work on the Early English County Court. In the sphere of the franchise jurisdiction, there is Dr. Lapsley's book on the county palatine of Durham, and Dr. Lewis's book on the Stannaries. In the sphere of central government there is Professor Baldwin's great work on the King's Council in the Middle Ages, and Professor Usher's work on the court of High Commission. I have already mentioned Thayer's work on the jury and older modes of trial. A more exhaustive and equally able account of the older modes of trial is Dr. Lea's book entitled *Superstition and Force.* Dr. Gross also made an important contribution to the history of municipal institutions in his *Gild Merchant.*

I pass now to general surveys of legal history.

General Surveys

Of the older writers mention must be made first of Wallace's excellent book on the Reporters. He has given us an account both of the Reporters and of their Reports which is unique. It is supplemented by Veeder's essay on *The English Reports from 1537 to 1865.*[35] Secondly, there is the series of *Essays on Anglo-Saxon law,* which, though published so long ago as 1876, is still useful. Of more recent writers four remarkable contributions are four essays printed in the *Essays in Anglo-American Legal History,* Robinson's account of the projected law reforms of the Commonwealth,[36] Dillon's essay on Bentham's influence on the law reforms of the nineteenth century,[37] Zane's five ages of the Bench and Bar of England,[38] and Veeder's account of the English judges of the nineteenth century.[39] The first deals with an important episode in English legal history, and raises the question whether it would have been for the permanent good of Anglo-American law if these reforms had been carried out. The second deals with a topic which Dicey has more elaborately treated in his *Law and Opinion.* The last two contain a most interesting account of that personal side of legal history which, as long as our system of law continues to be a system of case law, will continue to be of the utmost importance. Since it is to the genius and to the industry of great judges that many of the most original of the doctrines of the common law can be traced, it is obviously essential to know something of their personality and environment. Such surveys as Zane's and Veeder's, and such books as Wallace's account of the Reporters, give that human touch to legal history which enhances both its interest and its accuracy.

35 *Essays in Anglo-American Legal History,* ii. 123.

36 Vol. i. 467.

37 *Ibid.,* 492.

38 *Ibid.,* 625.

39 *Ibid.,* 730.

I pass now to the last of the topics dealt with by American legal historians — the sources of the law.

Sources of the Law

Pre-eminent among the American lawyers who have elucidated the sources of our law is Professor Woodbine. We owe him many debts. His little book on *Four Thirteenth Century Law Tracts* has cleared up the position in our legal literature of certain short tracts of the last years of the thirteenth century. His great work on Bracton is removing what has long been a reproach to Anglo-American legal scholarship. He is the first scholar to give us a clear account of the vast number of the Bracton manuscripts, to analyse them, and to base his text on the result of this analysis. We eagerly await his final volume, in which it is probable that he will give us an authoritative decision upon the vexed question of the extent to which Bracton was influenced by Roman law, and upon many other problems in the law of Bracton's day. His work is so good that we want more. It is good news to hear that he is also producing a modern edition of Glanvil.

Miss Putnam, whose work on the Statutes of Labourers I have already mentioned, has broken new ground in printing the text of Marowe's Reading *De Pace*.[40] It is very important new ground. If the manuscripts of other mediaeval Readings could be recovered and printed, they would

[40] *Oxford Studies in Social and Legal History*, vii. The book contains a full account of the early literature of the justices of the peace both printed and manuscript, an account of Marowe and his work, and the text of a Worcestershire manual for justices of the peace of the early fifteenth century.

be of the utmost value for the history of the mediaeval common law. They would show us the manner in which the mediaeval lawyers constructed definite bodies of doctrine from the Year Books, and would give us a contemporary or almost contemporary commentary on many of these Year Books. Lastly, I must mention Professor Beale's very valuable *Bibliography of Early English Law Books*, and his paper on the printed editions of the Statutes, which supplements and corrects the account given by the Record Commissioners.[41]

Before I conclude my survey of the ground covered by American writers, I must say a word about the work done by my friend Professor Hazeltine, the Downing Professor of the Laws of England at Cambridge. Though he holds Maitland's chair at Cambridge, he is still an American citizen, and so his very considerable contributions to our legal history should be mentioned at this point. He has done good work on the history of mortgages, on the Anglo-Saxon law, and on the early history of equity. His essays on Selden and Madox give us by far the best account of the achievements of these great legal historians; and his chapters in the Cambridge Mediaeval History on *Roman and Canon Law in the Middle Ages* break new ground for English lawyers. Of those chapters Professor Wigmore has said that, as a literary achievement, they are an unqualified success, and that, as an historical pronouncement, they are an enduring contribution.[42] The series of Cambridge Studies in English Legal History, which he has instituted and edits with care

[41] *The Early English Statutes, H.L.R.*, xxxv, 519.
[42] *L.Q.R.*, xliii, 118.

and skill, are a notable contribution to our legal history. The gift by Cambridge, Massachusetts, to Cambridge, England, of a Downing Professor of the Laws of England, we should regard as a part payment of the debt which she owes for the gift of John Harvard; and the fact that Professor Hazeltine and other Americans teach law both at Oxford and Cambridge, is a standing proof of the solidarity of the ties which are forged by a common language and common legal traditions.

I am afraid that this general survey of the work done by American legal historians has somewhat the character of a catalogue, and that it has the dullness of a catalogue. I can only say this in my defence: I could not otherwise do justice to the great debt which we owe to American writers. No mere generalities would serve. And so I rely on your patriotism to excuse the dullness of my narrative. I must now attempt to estimate the characteristics of this large literature.

(2) *The characteristics of this literature*

The characteristics which distinguish this literature can, I think, be summed up in three words — scholarly, practical, and liberal.

It is scholarly because it is based on a critical estimate of the best authorities, and upon an exhaustive acquaintance with those authorities. I think that writers like Holmes and Ames were some of the first legal historians to show, by their use of the Year Books, what a great light these Year Books could and should be made to shed on the history of the common law. The scholarly qualities of Woodbine's edition of Bracton are unsurpassed. Wigmore has mastered, without being mastered by, the large literature, English, American and foreign, of the law of evidence.

It is practical because it avoids the vice of antiquarianism. It deals largely in mediaeval law, and even in pre-mediaeval law; but the authors always have an eye on the end of the story. All the great books link up the mediaeval with the modern law, and show how the modern law has grown out of the mediaeval. And this quality is of the greatest service to legal history. It is an object lesson in its use, not merely to academic students of the law, but also to practitioners. In the memoir prefixed to Ames's *Lectures on Legal History*,[43] it is said of his work that, whilst " other lawyers have made the Year Books of the fourteenth century useful for the solution of some particular case: he made them the source of the most practical knowledge of current legal principles"; and that " the history of scholarship cannot show a better example of the value of applied history in present day affairs." This can also be said of many other writers on Anglo-American legal history.

It is liberal because it is a characteristic of American writers, more pronounced than in the case of some English writers, to stress the comparative and the philosophical side of legal history. A federal government composed of forty-eight states no doubt invites comparison more than our centralized judicature. However that may be, I think it is clear that, if you look, for instance, at Holmes's chapter on Possession in his *Common Law* or at Wigmore's treatise on Evidence, you will find that the learning is a good deal more

[43] At p. 18.

cosmopolitan than the learning of many English books. Your great real property lawyer — John Chipman Gray — wrote one of our best books on jurisprudence. I do not think that it ever entered the heads of any of our great real property lawyers to attempt a similar feat. But of this characteristic of the American contribution to our legal history I shall have more to say in the second part of this lecture — the foreign contribution to our legal history.

The Foreign Contribution

The fact that historians of Anglo-American law must draw upon foreign sources to elucidate our legal history, and the reasons why they must do so, have been so clearly stated by the editors of the *Essays in Anglo-American Legal History*, in the preface to their second volume, that I shall copy their words. "Many men," they say, "from many lands and systems, in time past, have shared in influencing our law. Bracton drew inspiration from an Italian, and Blackstone from a Frenchman; on Dutch learning Hardwicke and Kent were nourished; an Italian supervised the preparation of Domesday Book, and a Dutchman signed the Bill of Rights; Anglo-Saxon laws have been unearthed by a German, and Bracton's Note Book by a Slav; and a Frenchman made Bentham famous." The editors have acted on their belief in an "enlightened cosmopolitanism," and have included in their collection essays by a German and a Frenchman. Brunner has written on the sources of English law,[44] and Caillemer on the history of the executor.[45]

[44] Vol. ii, 7. [45] Vol. iii, 746.

Moreover, the same Association of American Law Schools, which initiated the *Essays in Anglo-American Legal History*, have done even more than this. They have initiated also the *Continental Legal History Series*, which introduces English readers to the best text books of many continental writers on many aspects of the legal history of their own countries.

At some periods in our legal history foreign influences have been great, and at others small. But I think that it is true to say that at all periods it is necessary to bear in mind analogous continental developments; for both the similarities and the differences often help us to understand the reason for the developments of our own law. In the first place, therefore, I shall say something of the reasons why, at different periods in our legal history, it is necessary to have recourse to foreign authorities. Moreover, foreign writers have sometimes made direct contributions to our legal history. In the second place, therefore, I shall say a few words as to the achievement of these writers.

(1) *Foreign influences on Anglo-American Legal History*

The twelfth and thirteenth centuries — the age of Glanvil and Bracton — are the centuries of the definite formation of the common law. It was an age of legal renaissance all over Europe. The school of Bologna was the most famous centre of the revival of the study of the Roman civil law; and in it originated the method of teaching law which, with some modifications and developments, prevailed for many centuries. From Bologna, too, came Gratian who was the founder of the mediaeval canon law. Now, at the very time when the study of the mediaeval civil and canon law was taking definite shape in Europe, England was in very close relations with the continent; for England was but one part of the large domains of the Norman and Angevin kings. It follows that the statesmen-judges who founded the common law could not remain uninfluenced by a legal renaissance, which was the most striking of all the intellectual factors of the day. It is obvious, therefore, that, in writing the history of this period in the history of our law, it is essential to estimate and analyse this influence. But, till quite recently, no attempt had been made to do so. We had only the roughest estimates of the most diverse character. Maine, for instance, said of Bracton's treatise that the whole of the form and a third of the contents were borrowed from Roman law.[46] Reeves, on the other hand, while admitting that Bracton borrowed the terms and maxims of Roman law, said that the actual doctrines borrowed would not fill three pages of the treatise.[47] It was not till the publication of Pollock and Maitland's history, and of Maitland's volume on Bracton and Azo, that any serious attempt was made to solve the problem. Maitland's views on this matter have been criticized as unduly minimizing the Roman influence. But we may hope that, at length, a definite solution will be reached when Professor Woodbine's great edition of Bracton is complete.

In the twelfth and thirteenth centuries, therefore, the assistance which foreign writers can give us is of the greatest value, because foreign influences on the formation of the common law were strong. From the thirteenth to the fif-

[46] *Ancient Law*, 82. [47] *H.E.L.*, i, 531.

teenth centuries foreign influences disappear, so that foreign books do not possess the same direct value. At the end of the thirteenth century the development of English law passed into the hands of a very close and a very insular profession; and both the institutions and the doctrines of English law were taking a form which were very different from those of the continent. But it would be a mistake to think that foreign books are valueless. They are valuable for three reasons. In the first place, we cannot understand the reason why England evolved some of the most characteristic features of her public law unless we know something of the corresponding legal developments abroad. Why, for instance, did the jury die out in France in the fourteenth and fifteenth centuries, whilst in England it became the most important of all the pieces of the procedural machinery of the common law? Why did the Estates General fail to stem the tide of absolutism in France, whilst in England Parliament succeeded in gaining control over taxation and legislation, and in becoming the greatest of all the securities for the continued supremacy of the law? We can not solve these problems without the help of writers on continental law; and, unless we can solve them, we shall miss much of the real meaning and significance of the English developments. In the second place, the continental developments in private law often help us to understand corresponding developments in our own law. We can learn much by contrasting, for instance, the manner in which Beaumanoir and Bracton tackle similar problems; and the significance of the treatment of the law of contract by the court of Chancery cannot be understood, unless we bear in mind the manner in which the law on this topic was being developed by the canon lawyers. In the third place, I think that we have something to learn from a study of the contrast between the way in which the civilians and canonists on the one hand, and the English common lawyers on the other, developed their laws. It is instructive to compare the methods of the schools of the glossators and the post-glossators, with the English mode of developing the law through the arguments used in, and the decisions of, cases. We have something to learn both from the resemblances and the differences.

In the sixteenth century — the age of the Renaissance and the Reformation — a consideration of foreign influences, and therefore the study of foreign books, is absolutely necessary to the proper understanding of the English development. How far was English law affected by the continental reception of Roman law? That was the problem which Maitland propounded in his famous Rede lecture on English Law and the Renaissance. Till he propounded it I do not think that English lawyers had any idea that there was any such problem to be solved. It is now recognised that it is a fundamental problem for the legal historian of the sixteenth century. It is not a problem to which we can give a short answer. But I think that we can say this: just as it was the rise of the modern state, and of new intellectual conditions, which, in many continental states, produced a reception of Roman law; so, in England, the same conditions produced an expansion of the common law; an expansion of the jurisdiction of many courts, such as the Chancery and the Admiralty, which exercised a jurisdiction outside the common law; and the growth of new courts administering new jurisdictions. Many of these rivals of the common law were more or less affected by foreign bodies of law, so that it is hardly possible to understand the principles on which they acted, or the new ideas which they brought into the English legal system, without the help of historians of continental law.

Three illustrations will make this clear. Take the large topic of maritime and commercial law, which is included under the title of the Law Merchant. The court of Admiralty, and later the common law courts, took over the law merchant as then applied in the great commercial centres of the continent. Hence, if we want to understand the origins of such topics as insurance, banking, or negotiable paper, we must look to the historians of continental law. Take the criminal law. We cannot understand the manner in which the Star Chamber went to work to rescue the country from the anarchy of the period of the Wars of the Roses, unless we bear in mind developments in continental criminal procedure. We cannot understand the changes made in the criminal procedure of the common law, unless we bear in mind the attractive influence of the procedure of the Star Chamber. Take equity. We cannot understand the manner in which the ideas derived by the mediaeval ecclesiastical chancellors from the canon law, were adapted to the needs of the day by the new school of lawyer chancellors, unless we study those principles, derived from the canon law, which that new school of chancellors had taken over from their predecessors.

In the seventeenth century we perhaps learn less from

foreign authors. The great constitutional conflict pursued its own insular course; but even here the study of the contemporary developments, which were all moving in the direction of royal absolutism, help us to understand something of the royalist point of view. In private law it was the period when a victorious common law was absorbing the lion's share of the commercial jurisdiction of the country. As Prynne saw, it would have made for a more intelligent and a more rapid development of the principles of commercial law, if English lawyers had studied the great continental books on commercial law.[48] But it was not till after the Revolution, when Holt became chief justice, that England got a judge who was alive to the importance of settling the new jurisdiction which the common law had acquired. It was not till the time of Lord Mansfield that English law got a judge who was at once a great English lawyer and a master of this foreign learning. We cannot understand either the strength or the weakness of Lord Mansfield, unless we remember that his learning possessed these two aspects. His strength in settling the commercial law and in putting the law of quasi-contract on its modern basis: his weakness in desiring to use this learning to unsettle settled principles of English law, in order to make them conform to what he considered to be the needs of his own day.

And then it must be remembered that, all through our legal history, there have been parts of English law which have been directly influenced by the Roman civil and canon law. Right down to the Reformation, and for some centuries after, the jurisdiction of the ecclesiastical courts was

[48] *Animadversions on Coke's Fourth Institute*, 133.

wide; and whether we consider their procedure, or some of the rules of substantive law which they administered, we must keep in mind principles and rules of the civil and canon law, upon which foreign authors can tell us much for which we shall look in vain in our English authorities. The history of international law, because it is international law, cannot be written from the standpoint of any one nation; and the same is true of Prize law, because it is a part of international law. It was because Lord Stowell was a profound international lawyer that he was able to create the unique system of Anglo-American Prize law.

Many of the writers on Anglo-American legal history, whose work I have surveyed in these lectures, have realised the need to take account of these foreign influences. Selden and Blackstone, Vinogradoff and Pollock, Holmes and Wigmore, and, as we shall see in my next lecture, Maitland, have all given breadth and an added significance to the facts of Anglo-American legal history, by comparing and contrasting them with the facts of continental system of law.

In conclusion I must speak briefly of certain foreign writers who have made direct contributions to our legal history.

(2) *Foreign writers on Anglo-American legal history*

The fact that English law is a very insular system has prevented many foreign legal historians from attempting to deal with its history as a whole, or with the history of particular doctrines. But it is not true to say that it has been entirely neglected by foreign legal historians. Ernest Glasson wrote a history in six volumes of the law and constitution of England down to the nineteenth century, which was published in 1882 and 1883. The account given of the history of legal doctrines is slight. But, when it was published it was, and, to some extent, it still is, the only book which sets out to relate the whole history of English law and English institutions. Brissaud, in his very complete history of French law, has, in many places, compared the French development with the development of the law both in England and in other countries. Dr. Juon des Longrais of the University of Paris has written a valuable book on *La Conception Anglaise de la Saisine du XIIe au XIVe Siècle.* The book is a remarkable study in comparative legal history. The Frankish and Germanic ideas on the subject of seisin are contrasted with the Roman ideas; and the author's analysis of the Frankish and Germanic conception of seisin, and his account of the fate of that conception in France and in England, present us with one of the most striking illustrations of the effects of the continued influence of Roman law in France, and the cessation of that influence in England, at the end of the thirteenth century. But I think that the two foreigners who have made the most notable direct contributions to Anglo-American legal history are Brunner, and more especially Liebermann. Of the contributions of these two great historians I must speak a little more in detail.

Brunner

Brunner is one of the great names in legal history. He is not only the historian of the Frankish period in the history of German law, but of much else besides. He was the first historian to state the now generally accepted view of the origin of the jury; and his papers on instruments made payable to bearer in French mediaeval law are the starting point of all discussions of the origin and history of negotiable paper.[49] At many points his books touch directly or indirectly on problems of our legal history. And, besides these contributions, he has written an essay in Holtzendorff's Encyclopaedia on the sources of English law. Till Maitland wrote his paper on *Materials for English Legal History* in 1889,[50] Brunner's essay was the only authority on that matter. It was translated by Hastie in 1888; and a revised edition of it appears in the *Essays in Anglo-American Legal History*.[51] It deals at some length with the Anglo-Saxon sources, and the Anglo-Norman sources down to the end of the thirteenth century. It then gives a much more summary account of the sources of English law down to the time of Blackstone.

Liebermann [52]

Of Liebermann it may be said that he has restored to us the authentic text of the laws of the Anglo-Saxons, and of the law books of that intermediate period which comes after the Conquest and before the reign of Henry II. I have said something, in an earlier lecture, of the beginnings of the study of the Anglo-Saxon laws in the Elizabethan age, and of the contributions of authors of the seventeenth and eighteenth centuries. Though that study declined at the end

[49] *Les Titres au porteur français du moyen âge*, *N.R.N.*, x.

[50] *Collected Papers*, ii, 1–60.

[51] Vol. ii, 71.

[52] Maitland, *Collected Papers*, iii, 447–473; Hazeltine, *L.Q.R.*, xxix, 387.

of the eighteenth century, it never wholly died out. Kemble, who was Grimm's pupil, was an enthusiastic student of the Anglo-Saxon language and laws; and the Record Commission published an official edition of these laws edited by Thorpe in 1840. It was not wholly satisfactory; and was in fact superseded by Schmid's edition. Liebermann's edition has superseded all others; and has gone a long way towards providing us with a complete text of the materials for the history of English law both before the Conquest, and also of that confused period which lies between the Conquest and the reign of Henry II — " a wild hinterland," Maitland calls it, " full of gins and snares, peopled by uncouth monsters." [53]

For this edition Liebermann examined about one hundred and eighty manuscripts in more than forty libraries in England and on the continent. He does not content himself with giving us a single text. He gives us in parallel columns the texts of all the leading manuscripts of the Anglo-Saxon laws, in the notes are divergent readings, and, on the opposite page, are passages from the post-Conquest literature based on these laws. As Maitland says, the book " looks like the full score of an opera." [54] And, in addition to the texts, Liebermann has given us an account of the former editions, a dictionary of Anglo-Saxon and Latin words, a subject glossary, introductions to, and a commentary on, the laws. The book is thus far more than a text of the Anglo-Saxon laws and Anglo-Norman law books. The texts are explained; and, in the glossary, the material is not only collected under appropriate headings, it is systematically

[53] *Collected Papers*, iii, 468. [54] *Ibid.*, 465.

arranged in the form of concise essays, which contain many relevant references to other Germanic bodies of law, and to other Anglo-Norman sources. It is, as Professor Hazeltine has said, one of the finest products of the new historical school of the nineteenth century.[55]

Liebermann was not only an indefatigable and well equipped editor of texts. He had, as Maitland said, "a good eye for men and movements as well as for laws and language."[56] Indeed, this is obvious to anyone who has read his essay on *The National Assembly in the Anglo-Saxon Period*, and some of his other essays and reviews. If he had lived, he could have written a history of English law before the Conquest in a manner and with an authority that no other scholar could approach. But we must be thankful for the large amount which he has given to us, and for the manner in which he has smoothed the path for that future historian. In his own sphere he was unsurpassed. May Anglo-American law be fortunate enough to find such another scholar — English, American, or foreign — who is willing thus to devote all his time and talents to the elucidation of the history of our law.

Both the American and the foreign contributions to the history of our law have broadened and liberalized the study of our legal history. Both have helped to make Pollock and

[55] "A new historical school, devoting special attention to the history of law, has grown up in Europe and America, into full and vigorous being, and has called to its aid philology, palaeography, diplomatic, and other sciences auxiliary to history itself. Liebermann has attained the foremost position among editors of Anglo-Saxon legal texts because he has been one of the leaders of the new school of legal historians." *L.Q.R.*, xxix, 391–392.

[56] *Collected Papers*, iii, 467.

Maitland's *History of English Law* a great book. That book sums up and states in a supremely literary form the results of the great historical revival of the latter half of the nineteenth century. The authors, in that history, said of Bracton's book that it was the "crown and flower of English mediaeval jurisprudence."[57] I think that we can apply that phrase to their history, and say that it is the "crown and flower" of the nineteenth century revival of historical studies. It could not have taken this position unless that one of the authors, who took the main part in its composition, had been a man of genius. Maitland, and the great services which he has done to the cause of Anglo-American legal history, will be the subject of my concluding lecture.

[57] P. and M., i, 185 (1st Ed.).

V

MAITLAND[1]

I SHALL not attempt to deal with the facts of Maitland's life, since they have been adequately recorded by Mr. Fisher.[2] Nor shall I attempt to enumerate in detail his books and essays — a marvellous output for one who in his later years was always suffering — as they have been admirably calendared by A. L. Smith.[3] I propose to say something, first, of Maitland's intellectual history and its results as seen in his books; secondly of his mental characteristics; thirdly of his personality; and fourthly of the influence which his work has had, and may be expected to have, upon English law and history.

(1) *Maitland's intellectual history and its results as seen in his books*

First and foremost Maitland was a lawyer. Mr. B. B. Rogers, in whose chambers he read, says, "He had not been with me a week before I found that I had in my chambers such a lawyer as I had never met before. . . . His opinions, had he suddenly been made a judge, would have been an

[1] I have adapted for the purpose of this lecture parts of a paper on Maitland which I contributed to the *Law Magazine and Review* of Nov., 1913.

[2] Frederick William Maitland, *A Biographical Sketch*.

[3] Frederick William Maitland, *Two Lectures and a Bibliography*.

honour to the Bench."[4] After he had left the Bar he used his practical knowledge of law and conveyancing to serve the interests of his college and his university; and, in all his work on legal history, we can see that his training in chambers and in the courts, gives an air of reality to his descriptions of the manner of life and thought of the remote ancestors of his contemporaries at the Bar and on the Bench, and a sureness of touch in his interpretation of mediaeval doctrine, and in his criticism of mediaeval documents, which could never have been learned from books. Professor Hazeltine says of Selden, "Undoubtedly his activities as a conveyancer, as an advocate at the Bar, and as a lawyer Member of Parliament, largely developed those capacities for accurate definition and statement, for clear and subtle analysis, for sound legal reasoning, and for judicial sifting and use of evidence, which we discern in his writings."[5] We see exactly the same characteristics in Maitland's work, and for the same reasons.

But, unlike most practising barristers, he was not content to be, as Sir F. Pollock puts it,[6] merely "a sound lawyer with scholarly tastes." His was a mind which would take nothing for granted, which was driven to analyse the causes and effects of all the legal rules and institutions, and all the political and social phenomena, with which he was conversant. Naturally he turned to history. In history alone could be found the explantions which he sought. History alone could show what was the original form of these legal

[4] *Fisher*, 15, 16.
[5] *H.L.R.*, xxiv, 207.
[6] *Quarterly Review*, ccvi, 406.

rules and instutitions, what sphere of usefulness they had once filled, whether they still performed any useful functions, and, if they did, whether by judicious change, they could be fitted to perform them better. While still a practising barrister he had been greatly impressed by Stubbs's constitutional history which he had read "because it was interesting"; and he so admired Savigny's *Geschichte des Römischen Rechts* that he began to translate it.

A sound lawyer, equipped with philosophy and history, and willing to use his philosophical and historical learning to criticize the technical rules of which he is a master, will produce some surprising results. The paper which he contributed in 1879 to the *Westminster Review* on the Law of Real Property showed that a new and peculiar star had arisen in the English legal firmament.[7] His use of Brunner's researches into the history of the English law of inheritance, to demonstrate that our division of property into realty and personalty was a relic of ancient barbarism, working mischief and injustice, which all other civilised peoples had long ago abandoned, showed what philosophy and history united to a technical mastery of legal rules could do for the cause of law reform. Long ago Bentham had wished to abandon the heir-at-law to the Society of Antiquaries. Maitland wittily suggested a more suitable historic hereafter. He was to be consigned to the "Gradualisten" and "Parentalisten" schools "who shall write monographs upon him to the end of time."

This paper marks an epoch in the development of legal thought. Most of the law reforms of the century had, up to

[7] *Collected Papers*, i, 162–201.

that date, been inspired by lawyers of the school of Bentham. Their simple faith in *à priori* principles had accomplished much in an age in which the legal system was in danger of being choked by the accumulated rubbish of centuries. But it could not accomplish all that they had hoped. It was a faith born of inexperience; and a larger knowledge of the complexity of human nature, of social problems, and of the technical legal rules which successive ages had invented to solve these problems, had somewhat dimmed it. Writers of the school of Maine were demonstrating that many of these principles were based upon a very superficial view of human nature; that they could not explain all existing rules even at the present day; that they did not even exist in the past. But the writings of the historical school generally stopped short at explanation. They showed how existing legal rules came to be what they are. They showed that even the most unreasonable of them once had a reasonable basis, and that some still had more reason than whole-hearted followers of Bentham's principles might allow. But that was all. Maitland's paper showed how history, in the hands of a first-rate lawyer and philosopher, could suggest practical proposals for law reforms, based not only upon a knowledge of existing law, but also upon a knowledge of the ideas which had created it. It showed that a knowledge of legal antiquities could be used, not only to teach old law and to explain present law, but also to suggest the changes needed to bring the present law into harmony with its modern environment.

And this was not all. Maitland's habit of analysing existing legal rules and institutions in the light of their history, enabled him to throw new light, not only on some of the most technical and difficult, but also on some of the most ordinary and familiar, features of our legal landscape. His critical mind was never dulled by familiarity. It was just these familiar things, which are generally accepted without comment and without explanation, that aroused him to investigate. And thus he gave us an explanation of the relation of equity to law, and an exposition of the great part which the Trust has played in our English life, which are as obviously true as they are strikingly original.

In 1884 Maitland abandoned the Bar, and became Reader in English law at Cambridge. It was during the course of that year that he made the acquaintance of Vinogradoff. Mr. Fisher, in his life of Maitland, has described what he rightly calls "the decisive meeting" of Vinogradoff and Maitland at Oxford on May 11, 1884 — decisive because it definitely determined the direction of Maitland's life work, and the sphere within which he was to exercise his great talents. Here is Mr. Fisher's description: [8]

The day was fine and the two scholars strolled into the Parks, and lying full length on the grass took up the thread of their historical discourse. Maitland has spoken to me of that Sunday talk; how from the lips of a foreigner he first received a full consciousness of that matchless collection of documents for the legal and social history of the Middle Ages, which England had continuously preserved and consistently neglected, of an unbroken stream of authentic testimony flowing for seven hundred years, of tons of plea-rolls from which it would be possible to restore an image of long vanished life with a degree of fidelity which could never be won from chronicles and professed histories. His vivid mind was instantly made up; on the following day he returned

[8] *Life of Maitland*, 24–25.

to London, drove to the Record Office, and being a Gloucestershire man and the inheritor of some pleasant acres in that fruitful shire, asked for the earliest plea-roll of the County of Gloucester. He was supplied with a roll for the year 1221, and without any formal training in paleography proceeded to puzzle it out and to transcribe it. The *Pleas of the Crown for the County of Gloucester,* which appeared in 1884, with a dedication to Paul Vinogradoff, is a slim and outwardly insignificant volume; but it marks an epoch in the history of history.

So great are the results when a teacher who is a man of genius meets with a pupil whose genius is equal to his own. The combination may be said to have put the study of the history of English law upon a new basis, and to have revolutionized the study of English social and constitutional history. The book which resulted from it showed lawyers and historians what could be learned from a set of records which, up to that time, had only been very occasionally used to illustrate isolated points in legal history, which no one before had used systematically as primary authorities for the social and constitutional history of England.

Maitland soon showed that he was even greater as an historian than as a lawyer or a philosopher. His edition of Bracton's Note Book restored to English lawyers a primary authority for the English law of the first half of the thirteenth century, which had been lost since the days of Fitzherbert. His work as Literary Director of the Selden Society gave the publications of that Society an immediate prestige, which made its future safe, and set a high standard to all future contributors to its volumes. His articles on Seisin and on the Register of Writs broke new ground, and showed as decisively as his contributions to the Selden Society's publications had shown, that from mediaeval law both interesting history, and information valuable to modern lawyers, could be extracted.

Then came the great *History of English Law.* In praise of that history much has been written, I shall not spend time in an appreciation of work which most of my audience are, from their own experience, equally capable of appreciating. At this point I shall call attention to two only of its many outstanding merits. In the first place, it gathered up the results of the nineteenth century English and continental and American revival of historical studies, and used them to construct a history of the origins of English law, in accordance with the exacting standards of modern historical scholarship. In the second place, because it dealt with the origins of English law, it elucidated the history of a period in which all previous historians were weakest. The authors say in their preface "Oftentimes our business has been rather to quarry and hew for some builder of the future than to leave a finished building. But we have endeavoured to make sure, so far as our will and power can go, that when his day comes he shall have facts and not fictions to build with." In fact, as I have said in an earlier lecture, this history, plus Blackstone, plus Dicey's *Law and Opinion,* give us an adequate account of the whole course of English legal history.

After the history came a series of monographs on many topics cognate to those dealt with in that history: — *Domesday Book and Beyond; Canon Law in the Church of England;* work on the Year Books. Later came works on the problem of corporate personality — the lectures on Township and Borough, the translation and introduction to a chapter of Gierke's great work on *Political Theories of the Middle Age,* the illuminating paper on Corporation and Trust; and his two excursions into the sixteenth-century history — the Rede lecture on English law and the Renaissance, and his contribution to the Cambridge Modern History. "Nullum quod tetigit non ornavit" — this sentence from the epitaph which Dr. Johnson wrote for Goldsmith's monument in Westminster Abbey is literally true of all Maitland's work.

Hale — the earliest historian of our Common law — once said: "That the law will admit of no rival nothing to go even with it." And so Maitland found. As his health declined and it became clear that his days were numbered, he devoted all his great powers to the history of English law. "Knowing the thing which he could do best, and judging that it was worthy of a life, he stripped himself of all superfluous tastes and inclinations that his whole time and strength might be dedicated to the work. Even music had to give way."[9]

What, then, were the mental characteristics of the man who has accomplished so much for Anglo-American legal history?

(2) *Maitland's mental characteristics*

The historical is sometimes contrasted with the analytic temperament — the mind which desires to know how a given phenomenon has originated, with the mind which desires to

[9] *Fisher,* 178.

explain the principles underlying the actual existing phenomenon. But, in truth, the great historian must have something of the analytic faculty, and he who would analyse must have the help of history if he would fully understand the thing to be analysed. Thus the historian, who wishes to trace the origin of some old rule of law or legal institution, must know something of its shape and content at the present day. If he does not know these things, he will not know what are the victorious elements, which he must disengage from the tangle of conflicting forces and tendencies, which he will observe in the far-off days when the rule of law or legal institution was born. To tell the tales of rules which never survived, of tendencies which were never realised, of institutions which failed, is mere antiquarianism. Effective legal history is the history of rules and tendencies and institutions which have survived because they were the fittest. But that necessarily involves a knowledge of what has survived. It necessarily involves a certain amount of reasoning from the established modern rule or institution to its unknown origin. Maitland, because he was a trained lawyer, was well fitted to pursue this line of reasoning with triumphant success. His *Domesday Book and Beyond,* and his introduction to the *Select Pleas in Manorial Courts,* are two out of many examples. After reading these books we feel that we have arrived at some conclusion — perhaps a negative conclusion, but still a conclusion. There are books, and learned books too, in which the author or authors seem to have been researching, so to speak, at large. Facts are carefully grouped, statistics are carefully compiled, theories are suggested, and carefully weighed. But at the end we are left very much where we started. To the obscurity of the original authorities the obscurity of a careful and elaborate commentary has been added.

It is exactly this sort of obscurity that a trained lawyer will avoid. If he has ever drawn pleadings he will have got into the habit of formulating an issue. And this habit, if he ever comes to write legal history, will be invaluable. There is a rule of law to be explained. We know that it had in its mature form certain characteristics. We see in the distant past certain causes which might produce them. We see other causes which would have given the rule a different turn. There is a clear issue — why did the one set of causes prevail over the other set? In answering that question we explain the rule in such a way that we see its connection with phenomena of social, political, or economic history, and restore the life that once existed behind the technical form. Thus technical forms are made to yield an instructive commentary upon the evolution of the social, political, and economic ideas which gave them birth. Legal history ceases to be merely the tale of the evolution of technical rules, and becomes a living history of the evolution of the nation's ideas upon all those matters which it considers to be of sufficient importance to be settled by the State. It is largely because Maitland treated legal history in this way that he made it a subject of such absorbing interest. He taught a lesson to succeeding historians of our law which can never be forgotten. What Coke said of Littleton we can say of him — "By this excellent work he faithfully taught all professors of the law in succeeding ages."

This power of formulating clearly the various problems

which arise in the course of tracing the history of any given legal rule or institution, enables an historian to know exactly what is the information he requires; and this knowledge is all important in a country where the wealth of original authority published and unpublished is overwhelming. It enables him to recognise the decisive authorities when he sees them. It enables him to emphasize the parts of those authorities which really count. Maitland was a great discoverer because he knew what to look for, and could recognise it when he found it.

But this method, though essential to the clear statement of the evolution of many points of legal doctrine, is sometimes dangerous. In the first place, because it involves the reading of history backwards, it is possible that we may read into the period which we are reaching in our backward career the ideas of the period which we are leaving. Some of Maitland's attempts to break up the primitive communities, of the earliest period of our history, into individual atoms, are based upon an analysis of the ideas of the thirteenth rather than of the tenth century. In the second place, it may lead us to start with a theory, and, having so started, to attach an undue importance to those parts of our authorities which support it; and this is a very subtle form of error, because it is possible to fall into it quite unconsciously. It is perhaps arguable that Maitland, in his Rede lecture on English law and the Renaissance, exaggerated the danger of the common law. That its supremacy was in danger I think he proves — but hardly that its existence was seriously imperilled. Again it might be said that, though all that he says in his book on *Bracton and Azo* as to Bracton's ignorance of large parts of Roman law is fully proved, too little account is taken of Bracton's use of other parts of Roman law — notably the law as to *dominium* and *possessio* — to which there existed more abundant parallels in the already ascertained rules of English law. But these are all very disputable points. What is not disputable is the freedom of most of Maitland's work from such errors. "Forewarned is forearmed." He was fully aware of these dangers as his paper on *The Survival of Archaic Communities*[10] shows. All teachers of early law and early institutions should put that paper into the hands of their students, because it affords one or two striking object lessons of some of the dangers incident to the use of the very necessary expedient, of arguing from what is known at a later date to what may be expected to have existed at an earlier date.

The skill with which Maitland avoided the dangers of this method of inquiry is, I think, mainly due to three very striking characteristics of his mind.

In the first place, none but the very best evidence would ever satisfy him. It was this characteristic which led him to turn from the task of continuing the history of English law to the task of making a critical edition of the earlier Year Books. Such an edition was, in his eyes, a necessary preliminary to the continuation of that history. It was this characteristic which led him to make, as a preliminary condition of fully understanding the Year Books, so learned a grammar of the French talked in the law courts in the fourteenth century, that M. Paul Meyer recommended it as a textbook to students of mediaeval French.

[10] *Collected Papers*, ii, 313-365.

In the second place, he had what we may call a concrete mind. It is easy, when writing of the history of legal theory, to state a doctrine and its evolution in general terms, citing perhaps a sentence or two which seems to illustrate the general statement. But will the statement bear the test of application to a concrete case? If it will not, it is clearly wrong or obscure. The most superficial study of Maitland's books shows that he always applied this test to his statements. In a letter which he wrote to me he said: — "People can't understand old law unless you give a few concrete illustrations: at least I can't."

In the third place, he is always alive to the human aspect of history. It is very easy when dealing with theories, and doctrines, and institutions, to forget that they were made and used, and developed and abused, by men of like passions with ourselves. Maitland never forgot this. He can extract human traits from a plea roll, and in his hands Year Books become human documents. He even invested his discussion on the Hide with some human interest, when he thus pictured one of the causes of "the phenomenon which has aptly been called beneficial hidation": [11] "Long ago the prevailing idea may have been that team-land, house-land, pound-land and fiscal hide, were or ought normally to be all one; and then the discovery that there are wide tracts, in which the worth of an average team-land is much less or somewhat greater than a pound, may have come in as a disturbing and differentiating force, and awakened debates in the council of the nation. We may, if we like such excursions, fancy the conservatives arguing for the good old

[11] *Domesday Book and Beyond*, 448.

rule 'One team-land, one hide,' while a party of financial reformers has raised the cry, 'One pound, one hide.' Then 'pressure was brought to bear in influential quarters,' and in favour of their own districts the witan in their moots jobbed and jerrymandered and rolled the friendly log, for all the world as if they had been mere modern politicians."[12] In both these last two points — in his love for the concrete and his sense of the presence of an all-pervading similar human nature — he resembles Walter Bagehot. These characteristics enabled both men to render ordinarily dull topics interesting, to give convincing explanations of abstract doctrines and tendencies, and to picture the characters and motives of men with wonderful skill and freshness.

Closely allied to this last characteristic of Maitland's mind is his sense of humour and his constant gaiety. His sense of humour, and his keen scent for the human, lead him to illustrate the institutions of the past by parallels from the present that, to use an hackneyed expression, both amuse and instruct. The quotation which I have just made from his discussion of the hide in *Domesday Book and Beyond* is as good an illustration as any. Innumerable instances could be gathered from almost any of his books. And this humour is never anything but kindly. It goes hand in hand with a gaiety of manner which makes light of difficulties, and often conceals the learning and research which underlie the brilliant argument that flows so easily. Finally, to this humour and gaiety there is added a talent for the epigram, which clinches an argument, and sums up in some memorable phrase the conclusion of the whole matter.

[12] *Ibid.*, 470–471.

(3) *Maitland's personality*

It was these mental characteristics which gave Maitland his extraordinarily effective literary style; and this style was an index to his personality. But the charm of the man was greater even than the charm of his style. I, to my great regret, never saw him. Two very kind and encouraging letters were all the personal intercourse which I ever had with him. And though his literary style enables one to catch glimpses of his personality, the testimony of many witnesses shows that no amount of diligent reading of his books can give the impression which he made upon those who were privileged to know and speak with him. "It is impossible for me," said John Chipman Gray, "to write or think of Maitland without recalling his personal charm. How great that was! I never saw him but once. But to have broken bread at his house among the Cotswold Hills will always be one of the happiest of my memories. If I said what I felt you would understand it, but to one who had not known him it would seem extravagant."[13]

Maitland was always ready to appreciate the good points of a piece of work, and he was always ready to assist and to encourage beginners. His passion for truth, Mr. Fisher tells us,[14] was so intense and disinterested, "that he would speak with genuine enthusiasm of such criticisms of his own work as he judged to be well founded, and to constitute a positive addition to knowledge." Such a man was necessarily a great teacher. Mr. Chaytor and Mr. Whittaker, in their preface to his lectures on Equity, say: "Those who

[13] *L.Q.R.*, xxiii, 138. [14] *Life of Maitland*, 177.

have heard them delivered — amongst whom we are — with all Maitland's gaiety and with all his charm of manner, and his power of making dry bones live, will not easily forget either the lectures or the lecturer. Equity, in our minds a formless mystery, became intelligible and interesting; and as for the lecturer there are few things that his hearers would not have done or attempted to please F. W. Maitland." And his pupils are not only those who were privileged to attend his lecture room. Many readers of his books have been induced by the charm of his personality, irradiating from his literary style, to interest themselves in the topics in which he was interested, and so to become his pupils in a very real sense. Maitland's personality, and the literary qualities of his work, will for many a year be an asset to the cause of legal history.

(4) *Maitland's influence upon English law and history*

What will be the influence of this great lawyer, historian and teacher, upon the study of law and history? It is too soon to judge yet. But it seems to me that in three directions his influence will be both far reaching and permanent.

First, he has taught us to apply the methods of historical criticism to the sources of English law. We know now something of the influences under which Bracton wrote. We know infinitely more than we did before of the real nature of the Year Books. From his various works we get many hints as to the point of view from which we should look at many other writers upon and sources of English law. It is good for a legal system to be taught occasionally to look at its authorities in a new light, because it tends to substitute for a blind adherence to their letter, a real understanding of their spirit. What the school of the humanist lawyers of the sixteenth century did for the study of Roman law, Maitland began to do for the study of English law. May there be found many successors to continue this work!

Secondly, he has taught English lawyers to look at their system in its relation to other systems of law. History, as he said, involves comparison. We understand the strength and the weakness of our own system the better for such a comparison. We see better where it is at fault. We are able to appreciate or criticize intelligently suggested reforms. And, at the present day, when physical science is diminishing the size of the world, and nations are losing their former isolation, such knowledge is essential. It enables us to learn from the success or failure of the legislative experiments of other nations. "The system of law under which we live, its merits and defects, its relations to other living systems, these are themes which — so I imagine — might and ought to have a place in a scheme of social and political education." His article on the making of the German civil code,[15] which begins with these words, shows how he would employ the comparative method, not only to elucidate legal history, but also to improve modern law. As Professor Salcilles has said: [16] "*Un ère nouvelle de rapprochement s'ouvra pour cette vaste communauté juridique que fut jadis l'Europe civilisée au moyen âge, et qu'elle redeviendra encore sous la pression des besoins économiques et civilisateurs de l'époque moderne. Si cette pénétration se*

[15] *Collected Papers,* iii, 474–488. [16] *L.Q.R.,* xxiii, 141.

réalise jamais, des hommes comme Maitland en auront été les premiers et nobles ouvriers."

Thirdly, he has renewed that partnership between the history of English law and the general history of England, which existed in the days of Lambard, Bacon, Selden, Spelman, Prynne, and Madox, but had, in more recent times, been almost dissolved. For the future we hope and expect they will begin again to carry on their business in common with a view to their mutual profit. Together they can accomplish much that neither can accomplish alone. It is obvious, on the one hand, that a knowledge of legal history is essential to the proper understanding of all branches of English history — political, constitutional, economic, or social; for the enactments of the Legislature, and the decisions of the Courts, represent the considered judgments of the nation upon many matters cognate to all these branches of history. It is obvious, on the other hand, that the reason which gives life to statutes and decisions cannot be grasped unless we know the ideas at the back of the minds of those who made them; and these ideas it is impossible to understand without some knowledge of the general history of the period when they were made. But, till Maitland pointed the way to re-union, law and history had remained too long in a state of unprofitable isolation. The lawyer, immersed in technical rules, forgot the human beings for whom those rules were made and the human needs which gave them birth. The historian, because he was ignorant of the meaning of these technical rules, was apt to misapprehend the meaning of statutes and the reasoning of the courts. Maitland showed how history can humanise law, and how law can correct history. He was a consummate lawyer; but he never forgot the human beings who made and worked the institutions, or the human needs which shaped the laws, which he was describing. Under his hands even the most technical rules became living things — the expression of human policy or logic, of human passions or ideals.

"The mark of a master," says Mr. Justice Holmes,[17] "is that facts which before lay scattered in an inorganic mass, when he shoots through them the magnetic current of his thought, leap into an organic order, and live and bear fruit." That Maitland was one of these masters is proved by his life and works; and, because he was one of these masters, the final verdict upon his achievement cannot be given until the age in which he lived has passed into history. I think that when the verdict is given it will be that in an age of great historians he was the greatest, that he was the equal of the greatest lawyers of his day, and that, as a legal historian, English law from before the time of legal memory has never known his like.

I have now surveyed in a summary way the great work which has been done by many men of great ability and by some men of genius, in the sphere of Anglo-American legal history. What, it may be asked, is the use of all their work? Has it any practical use, or is it only of academic interest? I shall conclude these lectures by attempting to answer this question.

In order to answer it we must consider first the value of history, and secondly the value of that particular branch of history which is concerned with the law.

[17] *Collected Legal Papers*, 37.

(1) There may be some who question the value of all historical studies. There were many who questioned their value at the end of the eighteenth and the beginning of the nineteenth centuries. As we have seen, it was an opinion held by continental thinkers, it was held by Bentham and his disciples, and it was not unknown in the United States.[18] It is true that the rise of a school of historically minded thinkers has demonstrated the impossibility of thus discarding the garnered experience of past ages. But, in spite of this, there may be some, who, looking at the manner in which the discoveries of the natural and experimental sciences have transformed the world by magnifying man's control over its natural forces, doubt whether the experience of ages, in which physical conditions were so different, can have any value for us today. Such a doubt is the mark either of a superficial mind, or of a mind so wrapt up in the study of some branch of the natural experimental sciences, that it has lost touch with those branches of knowledge which are concerned with human nature. No doubt the discoveries of science have altered profoundly the physical conditions of life; and an alteration of physical conditions must affect the lives and therefore the history of a people. But the course of history is not determined solely or even principally by physical conditions. That was one of the great errors of Buckle, who thought that the actions of man were as absolutely governed by physical laws as the properties of matter.[19] Physical conditions may change, but human nature reacts very slowly to the change. No doubt a change in

[18] See Pound, *Interpretations of Legal History*, 13.

[19] "I entertain little doubt that before another century has elapsed, the chain of evidence will be complete, and that it will be

physical conditions, spread over centuries, may affect the character of a people; but a rapid change of physical conditions leaves human nature very much as it was before those changes took place. If we look at the thoughts and acts of the intellectual leaders of men down the ages, at the philosophers of Greece or the lawyers of Rome, we may well doubt whether the human intellect has made much positive advance. If we look at the other end of the scale, and contemplate the follies and vices of mankind, it is clear that the animal side of man is always in evidence, and that constant war against it is the condition of a continuance of civilization. But, if this is so, it is plain that the lessons of history are as valuable to us as they have ever been.

External trappings may change; but the lessons which our forefathers learned in their age long war against crime and oppression, are still lessons by which we may profit. And, being lessons born of experience, they are of infinitely more value than the wholly original scheme of ingenious speculators. That, at any rate, was the opinion of Hale and Burke. "I have reason to assure myselfe," said Hale,[20] "that long experience makes more discoveries touching conveniences or inconveniences of laws than is possible for the wisest councill of men att first to forsee. And that those amendments and supplements that, through the various ex-

---

as rare to find an historian who denies the undeviating regularity of the moral world, as it is now to find a philosopher who denies the regularity of the material world," *History of Civilization*, i, 28 (The World's Classics Ed.).

[20] Criticism on Hobbes, printed in Holdsworth, *H.E.L.*, v, 504.

periences of wise and knowing men, have been applyed to any law, must needs be better suited to the convenience of laws, than the best invention of the most pregnant witts not ayded by such a series and tract of experience." "It is with infinite caution," said Burke,[21] "that any man ought to venture upon pulling down an edifice which has answered in any tolerable degree for ages the common purposes of society, or on building it up again, without having models and patterns of approved utility before his eyes."

(2) The value of that particular branch of history which is concerned with law is, I am inclined to think, of greater value than any other branch of history. It is of great value to all historians; it is essential to all lawyers; and, because it makes for the effectiveness both of the law and its administration, it is of great value to the state and its citizens. Let us glance rapidly at the validity of these three claims which I make for legal history.

Legal history is of great value to all historians. We have all heard of "key industries." Legal history is really a key branch of history. As Maitland has truly said,[22] if the history of law is not adequately studied, "the march of the whole historical army, and especially of those new regiments, economic and social history, will be seriously retarded. Whether we like it or not, the fact remains that, before we can get at the social or economic kernel of ancient times, we must often peel off a legal husk that requires careful manipulation." The reason is obvious. Law touches national life on all those many sides which the state finds it desirable to regulate, and so the historian of any of the

[21] *French Revolution*, 90. [22] *Collected Papers*, iii, 459.

important activities of mankind is sooner or later brought up against the law.

Legal history is essential to all lawyers. It is essential for three main reasons. First, if, like our own lawyers or the great jurists of the Roman Empire, they are administering an old system of law, they are being constantly confronted with old authorities and old rules, and interpretations of these old authorities and old rules, which come from all stages in the history of the law. A knowledge of history is obviously essential to the intelligent handling of these authorities and rules. Secondly, even if the lawyers are called upon to administer, not an old system of law, but a modern code, they need to know something of the history of the clauses of their code, if they are to interpret it effectively. The clauses of a code are often only the crystallization in a sentence of doctrines which have a long history behind them. We need to know that history in order to bring out the full meaning of that sentence. Still more do we need to know it in order to interpret it in accordance with the average layman's sense of right and justice. If laws are not made thus to correspond with the wishes of educated public opinion, they lose half their effectiveness — as Montesquieu said, " Laws ought to be so closely adapted to the people for which they are made that it is very improbable that the laws of one nation can ever be suited to the wants of another nation." [23] That is a recognition of the fact that

[23] " Elles [les lois] doivent être tellement propres au people pour lequel elles sont faites, que c'est un grand hasard si celles d'une nation peuvent convenir à une autre. Il faut qu'elles se rapportent à la nature et au principe du gouvernement qui est établi . . . Elles doivent être relatives au physique du pays; au climat glacé, brûlant,

national feelings and even national prejudices have a part to play in the interpretation and the administration of the law. The study of legal history can help the effectiveness of law, by enabling lawyers so to interpret and administer the law that due weight is given to these national feelings and prejudices, with the result that the ordinary citizen prizes it as a precious national possession. Thirdly, it is the study of legal history which is the most effective instrument for impressing on lawyers the essential fact that the maintenance of the supremacy of the law is the only security for the maintenance of both a disciplined and an ordered liberty, and of justice between man and man. It is because English and Roman lawyers have learned that lesson from their legal history that they have acquired that sense of the sanctity of the law, and the dignity of their calling, which are conditions precedent for the maintenance of high standards of professional honour and intellectual achievement. It is the maintenance of those standards and that achievement which have made Roman law and our common law the two great legal systems of the world. But this brings me to my third and last claim for the study of legal history — the fact that, because it thus makes for the effectiveness of the law and its administration, it is of great value to the state and its citizens.

It was the fact that English law was administered by an

---

ou tempéré à la qualité du terrain, à sa situation, à sa grandeur, au genre de vie des peuples, laboureurs, chasseurs, ou pasteurs; elles doivent se rapporter au degré de liberté que la constitution faut souffrir, à la religion des habitans, à leurs inclinations, à leurs richesses, à leur nombre, à leur commerce, à leur moeur, à leurs manières." *L'Esprit des Lois*, Bk. i, c. iii.

honest and a learned profession that was a principal cause for the reverence which Englishmen felt for their common law; and it is, I think, an admitted fact of English constitutional history that the continuity of that history is largely due to this reverence for the law. That fact comes out all through the Tudor period, and all through the constitutional controversies of the seventeenth century. Both the king and the Parliament professed to be acting in accordance with the law. No doubt they put very different interpretations upon the law; and this was inevitable, because the law itself, being at many points obscure, could be so interpreted as to favour very different political views. But both sides showed an equal respect for its authority. In these latter days the lawyers have less share in the development of the law than in past times. The law tends more and more to consist of enacted laws. Will democratic states succeed as well as the older lawyers, and as well as the governments of the old régime, in making laws which create in the nation a respect for law? The answer is by no means clear. Kings or aristocracies were always more or less conscious of the fact that they must, to some extent, conciliate public opinion. The majority in a democratic state, however small, because it is a majority, always imagines that it voices public opinion, and so can gratify its whims without further reflection. Hasty and ill-conceived legislation is the result, which tends to bring not only that legislation but the law itself into contempt. In England, a flagrant instance is the Trade Disputes Act, which emancipated Trade Unions from the control of the law. The experience which we have recently had of its effects has emphasized the need for modifying a measure which has gone far to sap the traditional English respect for law. You too, I think, are not wholly without experience of legislation which has not, to say the least, increased the nation's respect for its law. These experiments in this type of legislation prove that it is far easier to sap a nation's respect for law than to create it. And the reason is obvious. Respect for law is not a natural instinct. It is an artificial instinct which is the product of centuries of strong, wise, and honest rule; and artificial instincts need to be kept up to strength by the same arts as those by which they were created, if they are to withstand the assaults of the natural instincts of unregenerate men. This is one of the lessons which a very little legal history can teach the citizens of a state; and, if it could be learned, I have no doubt that the quality of the state's legislative output would be improved, and, as a result of that improvement, respect for the law would be increased.

In an age of rapid change, when the old mental and moral bearings of mankind have been cast loose, an engrained, and even unreasoning, respect for law is the most priceless possession which a community can have. It was this respect for law which, in the sixteenth century, helped the Tudor dynasty to carry England through the period of the Reformation and the Renaissance with less disturbance than was experienced in any other country. It was this respect for law which is the parent of many of those qualities on the possession of which English speaking communities are accustomed to pride themselves. Its maintenance is badly needed in the age of rapid change in which we are living today. Because legal history teaches us that its creation is the condition precedent to the attainment of a high standard of civilization; because legal history helps to create it by inspiring those who make and those who administer the law with high ideals; because legal history helps to maintain it by inculcating an intelligent respect for the lessons, taught by the past experience of our race, which it is its business to elucidate — for all these reasons I maintain that this long series of learned men, who have devoted their talents to this subject, have deserved well of the state. Let us all work for an ever increasing recognition of the claims of a branch of history which can teach Legislatures how to make laws which will command respect, which can teach lawyers the importance of maintaining a high standard of honour and learning, which can teach all citizens the lesson that respect for law is the life blood of civilization.

INDEX

COLUMBIA UNIVERSITY PRESS
Columbia University
New York

FOREIGN AGENT
OXFORD UNIVERSITY PRESS
HUMPHREY MILFORD
Amen House, London, E. C.

Bei Fragen zur Produktsicherheit wenden Sie sich bitte an:
If you have any questions regarding product safety,
please contact:

Walter de Gruyter GmbH
Genthiner Straße 13
10785 Berlin
productsafety@degruyterbrill.com